Reinventing Yourself

Life Planning After 50
Using the *Strong* and the MBTI®

SANDRA DAVIS BILL HANDSCHIN

app

Consulting Psychologists Press, Inc.

Palo Alto, California

Consulting Psychologists Press, Inc.
3803 E. Bayshore Road
Palo Alto, California 94303
www.cpp-db.com

Myers-Briggs Type Indicator, MBTI, and *Introduction to Type* are registered trademarks of Consulting Psychologists Press, Inc.

Strong Interest Inventory is a trademark of Stanford University Press.

California Psychological Inventory and CPI are trademarks of Consulting Psychologists Press, Inc.

16PF is a registered trademark of the Institute for Personality and Ability Testing, Inc.

ISBN: 0-89106-118-5

Printed in the United States of America
02 01 00 99 98   10 9 8 7 6 5 4 3 2 1

Director of Test Publishing & Information Services: T. R. Prehn
Senior Project Director: Diane G. Silver
Developmental Editor: Eric Engles
Managing Editor: Jill L. Anderson-Wilson
Copyeditor: Jean Schiffman
Design: Big Fish
Director of Design & Production: Laura Ackerman-Shaw
Production: Francie Curtiss
Manager of Manufacturing: Gloria Forbes
Manufacturing: Bunnie Finley-Livingston

Dedication

I HAVE BEEN FORTUNATE to have had many role models who have been vibrant, involved, and active in living their lives to the fullest. My parents, who at the time of this book's publication are 91 and 85, respectively, are my first and best examples. I admire and love them for the fact that they have always made choices based on their interests and values, never losing their curiosity about the world around them and never failing to thank God for another day to live and serve. Even as I write this they continue to balance four elements: work, learning, play, and relationships. Who says life choices end when you retire! They have quietly shown me that time is a wonderful gift and that choices don't stop just because the calendar shows the years racing by. This book is dedicated to them and to the loving and spirit-filled example they have set for all of us.

Sandra Ottsen Davis

TO MY PARENTS, ROBERT AND EMILIE, who were instrumental in leading me out into the world, who provided me with unusual and challenging opportunities, and who maintained a firm foundation of love at home. I watched my father struggle to find suitable "work" to give fuller meaning to his life after he retired from a lengthy career, and my mother struggle to survive that interim period. Ultimately, both were successful. Perhaps such a book as this would have made their transition easier.

Bill Handschin

Contents

CHAPTER 9

Achieving Balance in Your Life 107

CHAPTER 10

Experimenting and Exploring:
The Journey of Reinvention 125

Exercises and Worksheets

Figures and Tables

BEGIN HERE

Resist the temptation to skip this "introductory" material and plunge into the heart of the book. What we tell you here will help you get the most out of what you read later, and it may help you avoid some confusion about our intent.

Many books have been written for people over the age of 50, including a few about life planning, career changing, retirement, and finding greater life satisfaction. *Reinventing Yourself* is different. Rather than giving general advice about these issues, it makes use of two scientifically based tools—the *Strong Interest Inventory™ (Strong)* and the *Myers-Briggs Type Indicator®* (MBTI®)—that have helped millions of people better understand themselves and make wiser choices about work and relationships. These tools, or "instruments," can help you understand with greater clarity who you are, what you like to do, and what motivates you. If you have taken either or both of the instruments, congratulations—you've got a head start on your journey of reinvention. If you haven't taken them, don't worry—Chapters 2 and 3 are designed to help you approximate the most important pieces of information the instruments themselves provide.

This book is also different because it isn't intended to provide you with answers. Instead, it helps you ask the right questions—about who you are and what you really want to do with the rest of your life. And through this discovery process it helps you explore and evaluate the options available to you.

Why This Book Is for You

We're going to make a wild guess: You are approaching or have reached the age of 50 and feel your life is at a turning point. Perhaps your children have grown up and moved out, and you feel free of responsibilities for the first time in decades. Perhaps you have achieved financial security but the idea of "retirement" is scary or distasteful. Maybe you have "done" a career and want new challenges or a better-paying job. Or perhaps your marriage has ended or your spouse has passed away and you need to find new ways of making your way in the world. Whatever your exact situation, you probably have a sense that you now face new challenges and new possibilities; you see the potential for new beginnings. If so, this book is for you.

You won't find information here that is easily available elsewhere—such as advice about writing résumés and cover letters, "packaging" yourself to employers, or applying to educational programs. What you will find are ways to learn about yourself and techniques for using this information to chart a new direction. We want to assist you in making life choices that are congruent with who you are and who you have yet to become.

How to Use This Book

We have organized *Reinventing Yourself* so that it can be used flexibly by readers with different needs—those who have taken the *Strong* and the MBTI personality inventory and those who have not; people interested in a specific life issue (such as finding a new career) and those who simply want to explore. In any event we highly recommend that all readers begin with Chapter 1 and then read—and work through the exercises in—Chapters 2 and 3.

Chapter 2 introduces the *Strong Interest Inventory* and helps you clarify and explore your major areas of interest. Even though readers who have taken the *Strong* will be able to apply their results from their *Strong* Profiles, they will gain a better understanding of their interests by immersing themselves in the process of reidentifying them.

Similarly, Chapter 3 introduces the *Myers-Briggs Type Indicator* and allows you to make an educated guess about your personality type. Although readers who have taken the Indicator already know their four-letter type, they will gain a deeper appreciation of the unique characteristics of their type and how it differs from others if they work through the exercises in the chapter.

After reading these initial chapters, you will be ready to apply your knowledge in an exploration of the major areas of life: paid work (Chapter 4), volunteer work (Chapter 5), learning (Chapter 6), hobbies and leisure activities (Chapter 7), and relationships (Chapter 8). You can work through these chapters sequentially or begin with the one that piques your curiosity the most. Either method works. When you've finished reading the chapters of interest to you, you can contemplate the reinventing process from the broader perspective provided in Chapters 9 and 10.

Each chapter is built around a set of activities. Some are open-ended, reflective activities we've called *exercises;* others take the form of structured *worksheets* on which you're asked to record information and ideas. Both types of activities require active participation on your part, but we are confident you'll find the effort worthwhile. They will help you crystallize or bring to light what you already know about yourself and help you put it into a useful form. If you have a Profile from the *Strong Interest Inventory* and your results from the *Myers-Briggs Type Indicator,* keep these materials handy as you go through the exercises and examples in the chapters.

On the worksheets and on many of the informational tables, we have included descriptions of interest and personality characteristics. In most cases, the descriptions come from a combination of personal experience, knowledge accumulated from personal reading and study, and years of work with a variety of people in many different settings. However, we have at times drawn from the fine work of others in the fields of interest and personality. We would especially like to acknowledge the work of Sandra Hirsh, Jean Kummerow, Fred Borgen, Lenore Harmon, Allen Hammer, and Jo-Ida Hansen.

A final bit of advice: Even though you can use this book to launch your own process of reinvention without having taken the *Strong* and the MBTI, you will be working from a much stronger foundation if you do complete the instruments. The approximations of type and interest areas you can gain herein cannot replace the rich, accurate, and in-depth information about yourself provided by the instruments themselves. To find out how you can take the *Strong* or the MBTI, ask your career counselor, visit your local career center, or consult the list of providers in Appendix C.

REINVENTING YOURSELF AFTER 50

People who have reached the half-century mark are in a much different situation than people with less life experience. In their 20s, people feel the push of wanting to focus in on a single career choice and the pull of wanting to explore as many options as possible. In their 30s and 40s, they work hard to succeed in the variety of roles (family and work) they chose earlier on; they usually stay focused on becoming or being "successful."

In their 50s, however, many people find that earlier career and role choices have run their courses. They have a newfound freedom to make an entirely new set of life choices. They are wiser, more clear about their values, and relatively free of the expectations and imperatives that constrain people in earlier life stages. As one 55-year-old told us, "I am at an exciting and dangerous crossroad. I no longer feel that I have to *prove* anything to anyone. I feel much freer to express myself in my work and in my interests. There are fewer 'shoulds' for me now; I'll live the way I want to."

Many people at or beyond the half-century milestone, it turns out, feel they are at a crossroads in life. They are entering what Gail Sheehy (1995) in her book *New Passages* calls a "second adulthood"—a time of both endings and new beginnings.

As psychologists we have worked with many people making the transition into their second adulthoods. We have discovered, as have many others, that a successful transition requires a great deal of self-reflection—consciously reevaluating how your life works, evolving a new definition of yourself, changing old patterns, and exploring unexpressed aspects of the self. We call this process of self-evaluation and change *reinvention*.

Reinventing yourself isn't easy. Even if you have the desire to chart a new direction, it isn't always clear what direction will suit you best, fulfill your needs, and lead to the greatest satisfaction. What most people need to begin the process is greater self-knowledge—which is what this book is designed to help you achieve.

Standing poised at the edge of a second adulthood can feel both exhilarating and frightening. Being free of "shoulds" opens up new worlds of possibility, but it also means letting go of what is familiar and safe. At one moment you can feel extraordinarily confident knowing you can do anything you want, and at the next be shaken by a fear of being in limbo or discovering you have not made the best choices in your first 50 years. With this guide in hand, however, you have available tools that will help you experience the excitement of the crossroads you face and quell fears of the unknown.

New Possibilities for Your Second Half-Century

Being age 50 or older near the beginning of the 21st century is completely different from how it was for past generations. Economic, demographic, medical, and social changes have created a world in which the older segments of the population live longer, enjoy higher quality of life, have a greatly expanded set of options, and face fewer prejudices and expectations.

Expanding life expectancies alone have forced changes in how we think of the life course. Life is not forever, but it is likely to be much longer than many of us anticipated. Today, a woman who lives to age 50 without major illness can expect to see her 85th birthday. A man who lives to age 65 without heart attack or major illness can also expect to live to at least age 85. If many careers are 25 to 30 years in length, then at the age of 50 you have enough time for a second "career" if you choose.

And for those in the post-50 age group, roles and expectations are not nearly as rigid and stereotyped as they once were. Under the previous model, people went through three well-defined life stages: first learning in school, then working at a career, and finally playing in retirement. When you were in your teens and 20s and first dreaming about your future, didn't you assume that education, work, and retirement would follow each other in logical progression? Now, however, people have the option of mixing and combining the life activities of learning, work, and play in any order, of doing any of them at any stage of life.

For example, older people now have more work options available to them. Instead of being forced to retire and finding few open doors in the work world, people with decades of work experience are now actually being courted by many employers. The percentage of older workers nationwide is increasing as retirees enter new careers or work part-time in their former fields of expertise.

Perhaps the most dramatic evidence of how the old sequential model of the life course has changed is the extent to which people past the age of 50 are engaging in formal learning, the life activity that was once exclusively for the young. Go to any community college, community education center, continuing adult education office, or college and you will discover that education doesn't belong to any one age group. Older "reentry" students are one of the fastest-growing segments of the college population in the United States today.

Barriers to Exploring New Paths

Despite all these changes, old attitudes about retirement and aging persist. In our youth-oriented society, popular images of what it means to be old are often not very encouraging. Older people receive messages about slowing down, giving things up, or making way for the younger generation. Besides being prevalent in the media, such messages can also come from the people with whom we are closest.

For example, the mother of an acquaintance (we'll call him Tom) announced at her 65th birthday party her intention to take up painting and was met with incredulity by her children. In asking, "Why would you want to do that?" Tom and his siblings were really thinking, *Why would someone your age want to do that?*

People past the age of 50 encounter such attitudes every day. And when doubts about your capabilities aren't spoken aloud by others, they are often heard as persistent voices inside you. If you take these messages to heart, they can form barriers to your journey of reinvention.

It helps, of course, to recognize that our society's images of "old age" are astonishingly inaccurate. More and more, people past the age of 50 are shattering stereotypical ideas of what people their age and older "should" be doing. They are living differently, building new dreams, finding fulfillment in different places than before, and feeling free to be the people they want to be. They are living by a theme that could be summarized as "do what you love and don't worry about what anyone else thinks, especially your children."

Tom's mother, for example, blithely ignored her children's comments. Today, at 85, she not only finds great joy in expressing herself through painting but also has become quite skilled. Those doubting children now clamor for her works!

Because you picked up this book, we suspect you already know that popular images of the post-50 stage of life are stereotyped and based on *myths*. Still, myths can have a tenacious hold when you aren't fully aware of them as myths. With this in mind we'd like to describe in detail some of the more prevalent myths you're likely to encounter—or hear whispering inside your head.

Life planning is for people in their 20s or 30s; you're too old for this.

This myth assumes that older people have already lived most of their lives and made their life choices. While this may have been true several decades ago, it isn't now. As we've pointed out, people are living much longer and can expect to be healthier and more active during their later years than people were in the past. Moreover, so many more options are open to people past the age of 50 that life planning is needed to make the best choices. You can do almost anything after 50: start a new career, move overseas, raise adopted children.

I should build on what I have done in the past and not try to learn too many new things.

Did you actually like the things you did in the past? Were they activities that brought you the greatest sense of purpose or joy? The past may be something to celebrate or acknowledge, but it does not have to be what you repeat. And no matter what your age is, you can continue to learn new things; in fact, keeping your mind active through learning is one of the best ways of ensuring good physical and mental health.

Careers are only for younger people with full-time jobs.

Careers come in numerous shapes and sizes for all stages of life. A career really means a choice about roles and how those play out in one's life. What distinguishes a "career" from a loose series of jobs and role demands is intent and sense of purpose. In a career one has the sense of going forward, building on and adding to. Choosing to be a foster grandparent or working one-quarter time for a nonprofit agency can be called a career. Thinking about a new career at age 50 is as simple as asking yourself, What are and will be my major life roles? How might these express themselves in work, learning, and play?

We all have to retire sometime; making choices now is just a way to pretend the inevitable won't happen.

Twenty years ago retirement meant stopping work at age 65, receiving a pension, and taking it easy. Today, both the age at which you retire and what you do in retirement are much more flexible. What would you like retirement to mean for you? Are there ways of retiring that don't mean giving up involvement in the world and doing what you love? The many vibrant, active people who live full lives into their 70s, 80s, and beyond show us that "retirement" in the old sense is not inevitable.

The Four Circles of Life

When Richard Bolles, author of *What Color Is Your Parachute?* (1998), wrote his first major book about life planning in the 1970s, the old life-course model of learning in one's youth, working most of one's adult life, and then playing in retirement still had a strong effect on people. Bolles correctly saw that the sequential, rigidly defined nature of these three stages greatly limited people's approach to life planning. Since the three stages tended to trap people within them, Bolles called them *boxes*. In his book *The Three Boxes of Life* (1981) he proposed ways of breaking out of the boxes.

We want to take Bolles' idea and push it a little further. We believe the concepts of learning, work, and play are useful in life planning and decision making if they are considered not as stages or boxes but rather as interlocking areas of focus. Moreover, we believe a fourth concept needs to be added: the area of relationships.

These considerations lead us to a new model, what we call the *four circles of life*. We represent the four life-activity areas as overlapping circles because in real life they are intertwined and interdependent, even though each occupies a distinct role in life. This simple model of four circles, as shown in Figure 1, provides a context for life planning and for reinventing yourself.

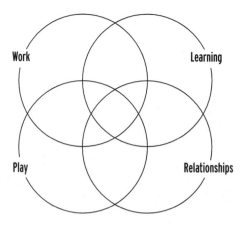

FIGURE 1. The Four Circles of Life

The four circles model also mirrors the underlying conceptual foundations of both the MBTI personality inventory and the *Strong Interest Inventory*. Among the 16 basic personality types described by the MBTI, 4 are most strongly identified with the area of work, 4 with play, 4 with learning, and the remaining 4 with relationships. Among the six basic people environments or occupational themes areas used by the *Strong*, two have a close connection with work, two with relationships, one with play, and one with learning. In later chapters we will explain how these correspondences play out and what they mean for your life-planning process.

Finally, the four circles of life provide a structure for this book. Chapters 4 through 8 are organized according to the four-circles model: Work (both paid and volunteer) is covered in Chapters 4 and 5; learning, in Chapter 6; play, in Chapter 7; and relationships, in Chapter 8.

Although we discuss each "circle" separately, our ultimate goal is to help you balance all four, to decide which to focus on at any particular time. Helping you achieve this balance is the explicit task of Chapter 9. Chapter 10 then goes beyond the four circles to consider reinvention as a process with six distinct stages.

2

DISCOVERING WHAT YOU LIKE TO DO
Interests and the *Strong Interest Inventory*

People differ in what they like to do. An engineer enjoys designing things that don't yet exist; a teacher likes helping people learn; a musician thrives on expressing herself and being creative. Each of these people has a unique set of *interests*—types of activities, challenges, and goals that are motivating and satisfying. This much seems obvious. It's a different matter, however, to measure exactly what a particular person's interests are and show in a systematic way how they differ from other people's interests.

John Holland's People Types

One system for measuring and categorizing people's interests was developed by John Holland (1959, 1965, 1973), who theorized that the world of work can be divided into six primary categories. Each category represents in one sense a type of person and in another sense a type of work environment. An occupation can be described by one or more of the categories, as can the people who work in that particular occupation and enjoy what they do.

Holland's categories are named Realistic (R), Investigative (I), Artistic (A), Social (S), Enterprising (E), and Conventional (C). Each category or people type is defined in terms of several unifying elements—primary interests, personality characteristics, values, and personal motivators. According to Holland's

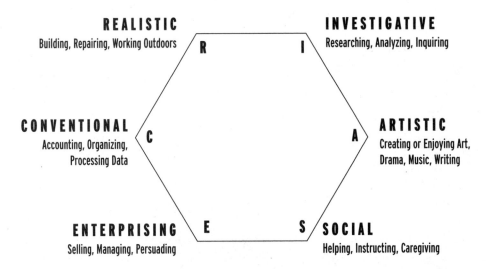

FIGURE 2. Holland's Hexagon

theory, a person is most likely to seek out (and be happy working in) a work environment that matches his or her interests, as described by the six people types.

The people types are interrelated in particular ways. To show these patterns Holland devised a model, arranging the types at the points of a hexagon shape, with related types next to each other and dissimilar types across from each other. You can see this graphic model, called Holland's Hexagon, in Figure 2.

The Social and Enterprising types, which sit side by side in the hexagon, are an example of a pair of related types. Both of them represent a drive to be highly involved with people in all aspects of one's work, although the drive is expressed differently in each. In the case of the Social type, the primary driver is helping and teaching others. In the case of the Enterprising type, it is influencing, leading, and convincing others.

The Artistic and Conventional types—opposite each other in the hexagon—are an example of dissimilar types. The Conventional type represents a drive to be involved with administrative systems, structure, and stability; in direct contrast, the Artistic type indicates a drive to be creative, bend the rules, and even work independently outside an organizational system.

We describe the characteristics of each type in more detail in Table 1. Many people are best described by some combination of two or even three of the types. For example, there are Artistic–Investigative people, Conventional–Realistic people, and Enterprising–Social–Artistic people. There are also people whose interests are so focused that they are best described by a single people type.

The *Strong Interest Inventory*

Long before Holland developed his theory of people types and work environments, psychologist E. K. Strong began working on a problem for the U.S. military: how to best match the innate interests of new recruits to the various military assignments. Based on this work he developed an inventory to scientifically measure people's interests. People responded to inventory items that asked about work activities, hobbies, and types of people; each person's pattern of responses was then compared to those of people employed in various occupations and satisfied with their work. The closer one's pattern of responses matched the typical pattern of say, accountants, the greater the likelihood that the respondent would be satisfied being an accountant.

Since its inception, the *Strong Interest Inventory* has been revised regularly (most recently in 1994) to ensure that it remains accurate, reliable, and relevant. In one major innovation, Holland's people types were incorporated into the *Strong* in 1974 under the name of General Occupational Themes. Since then, the Themes have helped describe a person's measured interests and organize the information provided by the inventory.

Table 1. The Six People Types

Realistic

Realistic people like to be involved in activities and jobs that are practical, action oriented, and tangible. They enjoy working outdoors and with their hands. Rather than imagining something, they like to see it, touch it, or manipulate it. "How to" books appeal to them; they tend to learn by doing. Physical activities and action capture their attention. Problems give them a chance to fix something that is broken.

A sampling of typical occupations
Auto mechanic, Machinist, Police officer, Gardener/Groundskeeper, Engineer, Building contractor

Investigative

Investigative people are driven to solve problems, figure out why things work, and understand the world around them. They are naturally drawn to scientific, technical, and mathematical problems or puzzles. Having time to learn about or study an issue appeals to them. They enjoy working with ideas by themselves or being around others who are learning, teaching, or studying.

A sampling of typical occupations
College professor, Science teacher, Physician, Medical technician, Chemist, Psychologist

Conventional

Conventional people are driven to create systems and structures for themselves or others to use. They enjoy devoting their attention to organization, detail, and accuracy and like working with numbers or data. They may particularly enjoy working with data that help them or others make investment or financial decisions. Being thorough and accurate has more appeal to Conventional people than taking risks or being creative.

A sampling of typical occupations
Bookkeeper, Accountant, Proofreader, Banker, Credit Manager, Dental Assistant

Artistic

Artistic people thrive on expressing themselves in words, art, music, or performance. They appreciate change and originality and enjoy participating in or being an observer of the arts. They tend to have a verbal bent and feel comfortable in intellectual environments and among people with unconventional lifestyles. They like to operate independently or at least have something that represents their own unique effort.

A sampling of typical occupations
Commercial artist, Reporter, Librarian, Art teacher, Musician, Technical writer

Enterprising

Enterprising people are driven to be in charge and to use their verbal skills to persuade others. They like setting goals and achieving economic objectives, and they need to see that what they do has an impact others. They may not mind being in front of a group and may like to be involved in politics. They enjoy participating in challenging activities and taking risks; they dislike focusing on details or performing laborious analyses.

A sampling of typical occupations
Realtor, Travel agent, Store manager, Buyer, Marketing executive, Restaurant manager

Social

Social people need to see that what they do helps or serves people in a direct way. Activities such as teaching, working in teams, and providing help or support to others appeal to them most. They are naturally drawn to those jobs that enable them to participate, belong, and work with others. They tend to be sociable, humanistic, and good listeners.

A sampling of typical occupations
Teacher, Social worker, Public health nurse, High school counselor, Occupational therapist, Speech pathologist

Source: Descriptions based on material in Harmon, Hansen, Borgen, and Hammer, 1994.

When you complete the inventory, you receive an interest-level score ranging from little to very high for each General Occupational Theme. Then your *highest* Themes are identified and summarized into a one-, two-, or three-letter Theme code. Each letter in your Theme code represents one of the six Themes, and their order shows you the relative strength of your interest in each. A Theme code of ESA, for example, indicates relatively strong interest in the Enterprising, Social, and Artistic themes and greatest interest in the Enterprising theme. In terms of Holland's people types, someone with a Theme code of ESA is an Enterprising–Social–Artistic type.

Since occupations (and leisure pursuits, types of volunteer work, and types of people) can be described by using the General Occupational Themes, a Theme code helps you know yourself. It gives you a springboard for thinking about occupations, educational goals, hobbies, organizations, and even kinds of people that are potentially congruent with your likes, dislikes, and inclinations.

Keep in mind, however, that a Theme code is just a summary of some of the information the *Strong* provides. Although very useful, it cannot substitute for your *Strong* results as a whole.

Finding a Theme Code That Describes Your Interests

Now that you've read descriptions of the people types (or General Occupational Themes, as we'll call them now), you probably have some idea of which Themes you gravitate toward. You might have even guessed a Theme code for yourself. And of course if you've taken the *Strong*, you *know* your Theme code.

Nevertheless, considering your interests in a systematic way—for the first time if you haven't taken the *Strong* and once again if you have—is very helpful. By carefully comparing elements of the six Themes you can decide which Themes hold the greatest relevance for you and why. Worksheet 1 on pages

16–17 will help you arrive at an estimated Theme code. If you haven't taken the *Strong,* this code will be a best guess at what the *Strong* itself would say; if you have taken the *Strong,* it will help you get back in touch with your interests.

Worksheet Directions

1. Notice that four different categories form the columns of the chart in Worksheet 1 and the six Themes form the rows.

2. Now focus on the first column, headed "Work Settings." Think about the items row by row. Which immediately grab your attention? Can you see yourself working in any of these places? Don't think about what you have actually done for work or what kinds of skills you have; just focus on what appeals to you. You may want to mark those items that are most appealing.

3. Repeat step 2 for each of the other three columns. For the "Potential Skills" column think about which skills you'd like to learn, and which abilities you'd like to develop; also consider skills you have and would like to use but haven't been able to use. For the "Self-Concept and Values" column think about what characteristics you admire and respect in others, not just what describes you.

4. Now you're ready to estimate a Theme code. Study your chart carefully, considering an entire row at a time. Which Theme or Themes seem to describe your interests the best?

5. If most of your interests seem focused in a single Theme, then the letter for that Theme can be your Theme code. If your interests are spread out over two or more Themes, decide which two or three best represent you and which of these is most important to you. Write your Theme code in the space provided at the bottom of Worksheet 1.

Your Theme code is a valuable tool. It says a lot about who you are and what kinds of activities you find fulfilling. You'll use it again and again during your journey of reinvention.

Remember that the Theme code you've derived in this exercise is only an estimate. If you have taken the *Strong,* this estimated Theme code won't be as accurate as the one determined by the inventory. If you haven't taken the *Strong,* we recommend you do so, both to get a more accurate determination of your Theme code and to take advantage of the rich information the inventory offers about your interests, personal style, and similarities to people in different occupations.

WORKSHEET 1. A Theme Code to Describe My Interests

	Work Settings	Leisure Pursuits
R Realistic Building, repairing, working outdoors	■ manufacturing ■ construction ■ engineering ■ utility industry ■ transportation fields	■ repairing old things ■ woodworking ■ repairing/restoring cars ■ refinishing antiques ■ hunting, fishing, rock climbing
I Investigative Researching, analyzing, inquiring	■ research laboratories ■ think tanks ■ colleges and universities ■ high-tech industry ■ medical institutions	■ working with computers ■ playing chess and other complex games ■ reading ■ outdoor research ■ going on study tours
A Artistic Creating or enjoying art, music, drama, writing	■ advertising, marketing ■ public relations ■ performing arts organizations ■ the media ■ law	■ writing ■ playing a musical instrument ■ attending performances ■ painting, photography ■ participating in theater productions
S Social Helping, instructing, caregiving	■ social service agencies ■ schools ■ hospitals ■ customer service ■ religious institutions	■ volunteering in a hospital or school ■ cooking ■ religious study groups ■ coaching ■ entertaining
E Enterprising Selling, managing, persuading	■ politics and government ■ marketing ■ sales organizations ■ independently owned businesses ■ fund-raising organizations	■ participating in local government ■ coaching ■ debate, lively discussion ■ entertaining and socializing ■ investing, risk taking
C Conventional Accounting, organizing, processing data	■ banks and financial institutions ■ accounting firms ■ computer industry ■ administrative support services	■ surfing the Internet ■ solving math puzzles ■ collecting and cataloguing ■ playing structured games ■ working in community organizations

WORKSHEET 1 (cont'd). A Theme Code to Describe My Interests

	Potential Skills	Self-Concept & Values
R Realistic Building, repairing, working outdoors	■ mechanical ability ■ physical strength ■ manual dexterity ■ athletic ability	■ practical, persistent ■ more at ease doing than talking ■ matter-of-fact communication style ■ avoid being center of attention
I Investigative Researching, analyzing, inquiring	■ analytical ability ■ objectivity ■ ability to solve abstract problems ■ computer skills	■ reserved ■ task-oriented ■ original ■ independent ■ analytical ■ intellectually curious
A Artistic Creating or enjoying art, music, drama, writing	■ facility with language ■ artistic skills ■ musical abilities ■ good at creating new things	■ creative, imaginative ■ humorous ■ verbally expressive ■ intuitive ■ romantic, free-spirited ■ nonconforming
S Social Helping, instructing, caregiving	■ teaching ability ■ capacity for empathy ■ listening skills ■ teamwork skills ■ verbal dexterity	■ caring, sensitive ■ humanistic ■ outgoing and cooperative ■ supportive ■ good team player
E Enterprising Selling, managing, persuading	■ powers of persuasion ■ negotiating skills ■ leadership ability ■ ability to delegate and manage ■ comfortable in front of a group	■ self-confident ■ verbally expressive ■ dominant, influential ■ achievement-oriented ■ argumentative
C Conventional Accounting, organizing, processing data	■ facility with numbers ■ organizational skills ■ time management skills ■ detailed-oriented	■ organized ■ controlled, self-contained ■ thorough, careful ■ task-oriented ■ conscientious ■ careful with money & materials

17   **My estimated Theme code**_____

3

DISCOVERING WHO YOU ARE
Personality Type and the MBTI

Do you enjoy constant social interaction, or do you need time alone to recharge your batteries? Are you comfortable making top-level decisions, or do you prefer leaving such responsibilities to others? Do you like to live a structured and organized life or be spontaneous and flexible? We all know that personalities are different and unique, that each person has a particular set of natural inclinations, likes, dislikes, needs, and strengths. What we often don't fully recognize is the connection between our personalities and how much we enjoy working in a certain job, assuming a certain role, or interacting with a certain person. If you thrive on social interaction, you won't be happy holed up in an office all day. If you need structure in your life, a fluid environment may drive you crazy. You'll be happiest if your personality—who you are—fits with what you do.

Learning more about who you are, then, is a key step in finding greater happiness in the second half of your life—the right work role, fulfilling activities, satisfying relationships. In this chapter, you take this important step by discovering which of the 16 personality types defined by the *Myers-Briggs Type Indicator* describes your personality the best. Knowing your type, you are better prepared to make conscious choices about how to express each part of your personality in your life. If you already have results from the MBTI, we invite you to read this short chapter as a way of refamiliarizing yourself with your preferences and reconnecting with what makes you tick.

The *Myers-Briggs Type Indicator* and the Four Preferences

The *Myers-Briggs Type Indicator* (MBTI) combines the personality theory of Swiss psychologist C. G. Jung with the empirical work of two Americans, Katharine Cook Briggs and her daughter, Isabel Briggs Myers. Briggs was studying differences in people's personalities in the early 1920s when she read Jung's newly published book on personality types. Jung theorized that personality is made up of elements that, like single coins, each have two opposite sides. A person is naturally inclined to favor one side of each element or the other, said Jung, even though he or she will use both sides some of the time.

Finding Jung's theory insightful, Briggs, together with Isabel Briggs Myers, expanded on Jung's theoretical model. Then Briggs and Myers began focusing on giving the theory a practical application, an effort that led to the development of the MBTI personality inventory in the 1940s. Since then, the instrument has been refined and improved many times, most recently in 1998.

The MBTI deals with four fundamental dimensions of human personality: how we take in information, how we make decisions, how we gain energy, and how we orient ourselves to the external world. Each dimension is made up of two opposite poles, and is called a *dichotomy.* For each dichotomy, a person has a *preference* for one pole or the other.

Your preferences are your home bases—what you tend to do naturally or what you gravitate toward when there are no particular external demands for you to operate one way or the other. Using your preferences feels easy and comfortable.

Table 2 shows the four dichotomies and their opposite poles. Soon you'll complete a worksheet to estimate which poles you prefer. Notice that each preference is represented by its

Table 2. The Four MBTI Dichotomies

Ways of Gaining Energy

Extraversion (E)		**Introversion (I)**
Focusing on the outside world and getting energy by interacting with people and being active	vs.	Focusing on one's inner world and getting energy by reflecting on ideas and experiences and having time alone

Ways of Taking in Information

Sensing (S)		**Intuition (N)**
Noticing and trusting facts, specifics, past experience, and present realities	vs.	Using imagination and trusting patterns and future possibilities

Ways of Making Decisions

Thinking (T)		**Feeling (F)**
Using logical analysis, objectivity, and intellectual criteria	vs.	Using values, feelings, and subjective criteria

Ways of Living in the World

Judging (J)		**Perceiving (P)**
Preferring structure, organization, preparation, and closure	vs.	Preferring flexibility, spontaneity, and keeping options open as long as possible

first letter (except in the case of Intuition, where N is used to distinguish it from Introversion).

Your preference for a pole of a dichotomy can range from very clear to slight. If you have a clear preference for one pole, you will easily gravitate toward behaviors that express it.

Each of your preferences works in concert with the others to form a whole—your personality type—that is greater than the sum of the parts. Your individual preferences, however, are used to name or identify your type. For example, if your preferences are for Extraversion, Sensing, Feeling, and Judging, then your type is ESFJ. There are 16 types because there are 16 ways of combining preferences in the four dichotomies. The different types, arranged in the way Myers and Briggs originally thought of them, are shown in Table 3.

Table 3. The 16 MBTI Types

ISTJ	ISFJ	INFJ	INTJ
ISTP	ISFP	INFP	INTP
ESTP	ESFP	ENFP	ENTP
ESTJ	ESFJ	ENFJ	ENTJ

Each personality type has unique gifts. No type is "better" than any of the others. Type has nothing to do with intelligence or psychological health.

Even though every person fits into one of 16 types, type does not cover all individual variations. Two people with the same type have much in common, but they also differ in many ways. Each person expresses his or her preferences in a unique way. One can't predict a person's behavior just by knowing his or her type.

Your preferences are with you for your entire life, but the way you use them goes through a natural process of development and change. Early in life a person learns to express his or her four major gifts. Extraverted types play to their gift of giving voice to their thoughts; Introverted types focus on their gift for reflection. Later in life, with preferences firmly established, a person may experiment with using the opposite, nonpreferred side of each dichotomy for balance. The Extravert learns to value private time and the Introvert seeks more energy from contact with others.

For many people the stage of life after age 50 is a time when this process of type development comes to the fore. More aware of their natural gifts, they realize that expanding their personalities can be a challenge that brings fulfillment and renewal. For example, a 52-year-old executive with a preference for Judging explained that she was experimenting with a Perceiving approach: "I've always run my life with plans, agendas, and careful preparation, but now I'm finding great joy in doing some things spontaneously. Frankly, my staff finds it unnerving, but I think it's great."

In the chapters that follow you will be considering how much you wish to play to your natural gifts in what you choose to do. You may continue to draw on the gifts you already have, or you may choose the more difficult road of learning to express your opposite, less-preferred modes.

Your MBTI Type

Worksheet 2 on pages 25–26 will help you determine where your preferences likely lie. If you haven't taken the MBTI personality inventory, you may already have started to figure out what fits for you. The worksheet, however, will help you make a more accurate estimate because it has you consider elements of each dichotomy separately. (Keep in mind, though, that the only way to be sure about your type is to contact a professional and complete the MBTI.) If you have taken the MBTI and know your type, working through the worksheet will help reacquaint you with your preferences and the unique way in which you express each one.

To be most accurate on the worksheet, think only about what you know about yourself and what you prefer, not what you do (what you do is influenced by your environment and may not reflect your actual preferences). Your goal is to identify and reaffirm your gifts. Later we'll look at exploring your opposites.

Worksheet Directions

1. Look at the chart in Worksheet 2 for the Extraversion–Introversion dichotomy, called "What is my source of energy?" Each row of the chart describes two opposite aspects of this dichotomy. Consider the choice presented by the first row: Do you tend to be energized by people and events or by having time alone with your own thoughts and feelings? Which of these statements describes you best?

2. Repeat this process for the other rows of the chart. Sometimes you will know right away which of the two opposing statements describes you best. For others, you will be less certain.

3. When you've finished with all the rows, make an evaluation of your overall preference for that dichotomy. You can give extra weight to a row if your preference in that row is particularly clear.

4. Repeat steps 1−3 for each of the other dichotomies.

When you've estimated all four of your preferences, write the four letters that represent each of them in the spaces below.

____	____	____	____
E or I	**S or N**	**T or F**	**J or P**

If you've taken the MBTI, how do your results match with these? If there is a difference, look at the dichotomies in which there is disagreement and examine the choices you made in the exercise. Do the choices for the opposite preference make sense too?

If you haven't taken the MBTI, you may want to read the description for your estimated type in Appendix A. Does the description fit you well? If it is not quite a match and you are unsure about any of your preferences, read the descriptions for your other possible types and decide which fits you best. Or, even better, find a local provider of the MBTI in Appendix C and take the actual inventory.

WORKSHEET 2. My Estimated Preferences

What is my source of energy?

Extraversion (E)	Introversion (I)
■ Energized by people and external events	■ Energized by time alone with my thoughts
■ Talkative and expressive	■ Talk when I can improve on silence
■ Focused primarily on the outside world	■ Focused primarily on my internal world
■ Like to talk things out	■ Like to think things through
■ Enjoy knowing a little about many topics	■ Enjoy knowing a few topics in depth
■ Tend to act first and think second	■ Tend to think first and act second
■ Become bored with too much time alone	■ Need time alone for relaxation
■ Interactive, energetic	■ Reflective, thoughtful
■ Always ready to fill my time with people	■ Thrive on having activities I can do alone

How do I take in information?

Sensing (S)	Intuition (N)
■ Pay attention to my senses	■ Pay attention to my imagination
■ Stay close to reality	■ Imagine future possibilities
■ Practical; look for what will work	■ Creative; look for possibilities
■ Like to know about the details	■ Like to see the big picture
■ Value what has worked in the past	■ Value change and innovation
■ Realistic; know what is possible	■ Imaginative; dream about what could be
■ Oriented toward the present	■ Oriented toward the future
■ Like to be factual and literal	■ Like to be general and figurative
■ Want to see specific how-to steps	■ Want to know the general idea or pattern

How do I decide?

Thinking (T)	Feeling (F)
■ Use logic; consider pros and cons	■ Consider values and how decisions affect people
■ Value truth and objectivity	■ Value compassion and sensitivity
■ Discover my feelings by thinking about them	■ Experience the world through my feelings
■ Want people to be treated fairly	■ Want people to live in harmony
■ Tend to see flaws and be evaluative	■ Tend to be appreciative and complimentary
■ Judge myself by what I do or achieve	■ Value myself for who I am
■ Sometimes don't notice others' emotions	■ Quickly sense others' underlying feelings
■ Seek debate and constructive conflict	■ Seek harmony and avoid conflict

How do I like to live in the world?

Judging (J)	Perceiving (P)
■ Can relax when there is a plan	■ Feel uncomfortable when things are too planned out
■ Like structure and closure	■ Like spontaneity and flexibility
■ Believe the world needs to be controlled	■ Believe the world should be experienced
■ Prefer to be prepared in advance	■ Like the excitement of the last minute
■ Disciplined, predictable	■ Responsive, adaptable
■ Develop agendas and lists	■ Create lists but lose them
■ Make up my mind quickly	■ Want to be sure I know all the options
■ Tend to live a planned life	■ Tend to live a flexible life
■ May experience Perceiving types as disorganized	■ May experience Judging types as controlling

Source: Based in part on Myers, 1993.

4

TRANSFORMING YOUR WORK LIFE— PAID WORK

If you can't wait to go to work each day, if your work life is completely fulfilling as it is, then this chapter probably isn't for you. If, however, you want change in your work situation—whether to follow your passion, to secure a higher-paying job, to devote more time or less time to work, or to begin working again after being unemployed—then this chapter may help you reinvent the first circle of your life.

Our focus here is on direction setting: helping you set criteria for mapping out avenues of exploration for the second half of your life. We don't try to assist you in the process of getting hired, except to offer the listing of job-search resources in Appendix B.

Finding satisfying new work that matches your personality and interests requires self-knowledge. You need to peel away the "shoulds," the old habits, the expectations of others, and discover, deep down, what really motivates you. You need to contemplate with whom you like to work and what has caused frustration with work in the past. Identifying your interests and skills, taking your daydreams seriously, and even remembering your childhood fantasies are all ways of getting to know yourself better and pointing yourself in the direction of new work activities.

This chapter combines self-discovery exercises with exercises based on the *Strong Interest Inventory* and your *Myers-Briggs Type Indicator* preferences. These exercises will help you get a clearer picture of what has been or could be compelling and satisfying to you. Once you have worked through the exercises, you will have a blueprint you can use to identify paid work opportunities and evaluate how well different options match your interests, skills, values, and personality.

Remember that the work circle of life includes both paid work and volunteer work. The following chapter, on working as volunteer, contains a variety of self-discovery exercises you may find helpful in searching for paid work that better meets your needs. Similarly, what you learn about yourself in this chapter may apply equally well to finding satisfying volunteer work.

Tapping In to Your Deeper Self

What would you do if you could? What's your fantasy? When people answer these questions, they often think their responses are unimportant. They shrug them off as impractical, impossible, or mere flights of fancy. Yet answers to questions such as these hold some truth about who a person really is and offer clues to what is rarely brought to a conscious level.

Pay attention to the voice inside you that speaks for these "impractical" yearnings. Don't let its softer volume get drowned out by the other, louder voices competing for your attention. Exercises 1 through 3 may help you hear that voice.

Spend as much or as little time as you like with these exercises and do them in your own way. You may want to record your impressions in depth in a journal, make a short list of responses, or just sit and think. Or you may want to pair up with a friend and talk through your experiences. You can spend hours on each exercise or only a few minutes.

Now take a few minutes to reflect on what you discovered through these exercises. We suggest this strategy: Review the description of each of the General Occupational Themes in your

EXERCISE 1: Childhood Dreams

When you were a child, what did you want to be when you grew up? Think back to some of the first things you daydreamed about. What kinds of work got your imagination going? Whom did you admire? What appealed to you most about these dreams?

EXERCISE 2: Peak Experiences

Each of us has had moments when we felt on top of the world, completely unself-conscious, especially competent. These peak experiences occur when we are using our gifts. Reflect back on each period of your life—childhood, teens, 20s, 30s, and so on. For each stage or decade, think about what stand out as peak experiences, whether they lasted for a few minutes or a few months. List as many as possible. Then for each experience identify the key aspects of the situation: What were you doing that was so enjoyable and right? With whom were you doing it? What was the place and context? What values were involved?

EXERCISE 3: When Time Flies

Have you ever had the experience of not noticing how much time has gone by? What are you doing when that happens? What is it that you lose yourself in? What kinds of things are so enjoyable that you will do them whenever you can? Imagine having a chance every day to be lost in some of the things you love.

Theme code in Chapter 2 (see Worksheet 1 on pages 16–17 and Table 1 on page 12). For each category ("Work Settings," "Leisure Pursuits," etc.), consider your reflections on your childhood dreams and peak experiences. What additional areas of interest have they revealed? What do they suggest about areas of particular importance to you?

You may want to make a table modeled on the following one for recording what you've learned:

	Most appealing items from the Themes in my Theme code	**Additional items discovered by tapping in to my deeper self**
Work settings		
Leisure pursuits		
Potential skills		
Self-concept and values		

Zeroing In on Work Activities: The Basic Interest Scales

The General Occupational Themes (GOTs) in which you have the most interest—summarized by your Theme code—provide helpful guidelines for directing your search for new work. Somewhat more specific guidance is provided by the *Strong's* Basic Interest Scales. These scales (we'll call them basic interest *areas*) group together similar kinds of activities and are often linked directly to actual job positions and careers. Their value lies in helping you decide which interests you need to express in your life to feel fulfilled.

Each of us has a primary pattern of interests that tends to be stable over time. However, in midlife some areas may become more intriguing and others may lose their earlier attraction. You may get tired of a type of work activity or develop some newfound hobby or passion, even though the majority of what you loved in your late 20s remains the same.

Second adulthood can be a time to explore and experiment. What have you wished you could do that you have been reluctant to try? What interest or activity has "run its course"? What have you been involved in off the job that is such a great passion that it could form the focus for your next paid work opportunity? Evaluating your attraction to each of the basic interest areas can help you answer these questions.

There are a total of 25 Basic Interest Scales on the *Strong*, each grouped under one of the General Occupational Themes. When you take the *Strong*, your results on these scales are presented in the same way as your results on the GOTs. Your scores—from very low to very high—show how much each of the activities attracts you.

Worksheet 3 on pages 33–34 lists all of the basic interest areas included in the *Strong*. If you haven't taken the *Strong*, you can use the worksheet to estimate your level of interest in each of the 25 basic interest areas. If you have taken the inventory, we recommend completing the worksheet without first looking at your *Strong* Profile. Then you can compare your *Strong* results with your worksheet ratings. The scoring of the Basic Interest Scales on the *Strong* is rather complex and based on comparisons with a large sample of people, but your estimates of your interest levels should roughly correspond with your *Strong* scores.

You'll notice the worksheet has a dual purpose. You will work through it twice: The first time, you'll consider how much each activity area appeals to you; the second time (as a separate exercise, described in the next section), you will rate how confident you are of your skills in each area. After you have done both ratings, you will fill in a chart that suggests courses of action in relation to each area of interest.

Worksheet Directions

1. Assess your level of interest in each of the basic interest areas listed on Worksheet 3. Try not to be unduly influenced by previous experience in an area or lack of it. Similarly, don't consider whether you have talent in an area or whether you have the ability to learn the skills in the area. Just focus on your attraction to the area and its activities. Think of the basic interest areas as magnets: Some attract you and others make you want to turn away.

2. Rate your level of interest in each area by marking the appropriate box in the center "Level of interest" column. Use the following rating scale:

(Highest interest) 5   I really love everything related to this area
4   I would like to spend time at these activities
3   The activities in the area are somewhat appealing
2   I'd rather not get involved in these activities
(Lowest interest) 1   I want to avoid this area entirely

Ignore the right-hand column for now.

Before you move on to the next exercise, reflect on what you have discovered so far about your basic interests. Have you found any areas of basic interest outside of your Themes of highest interest? Which of your basic interests do you think needs an outlet in your paid work? Which basic interests have never had an outlet? What activities are you involved in right now that don't match your passions?

Remember that there is a difference between having an interest and expressing it. Just because you are intrigued by a kind of activity doesn't mean you should get involved in it. Once you know your interests, you have a choice to make about how, when, and whether to express them.

Similarly, your current behavior may not reflect your interests. Habits are powerful! You may be involved in some activities simply because you haven't thought about *not* doing them. Being involved and moderately interested does not mean you have to continue with an activity. Use your knowledge of what you like and what you express now to help you think about the changes you want to make.

WORKSHEET 3. My Basic Interests

Basic Interest Area	Level of Interest					Level of Confidence in My Skills				
	5	4	3	2	1	5	4	3	2	1
AGRICULTURE (R)—farming or ranching; working with plants or animals	❑	❑	❑	❑	❑	❑	❑	❑	❑	❑
NATURE (R)—appreciating natural beauty and being outdoors	❑	❑	❑	❑	❑	❑	❑	❑	❑	❑
MILITARY ACTIVITIES (R)—drilling and training in a structured environment	❑	❑	❑	❑	❑	❑	❑	❑	❑	❑
ATHLETICS (R)—watching or taking part in sports or athletics	❑	❑	❑	❑	❑	❑	❑	❑	❑	❑
MECHANICAL ACTIVITIES (R)—repairing mechanical things or working with machines	❑	❑	❑	❑	❑	❑	❑	❑	❑	❑
SCIENCE (I)—doing scientific research; studying the physical sciences	❑	❑	❑	❑	❑	❑	❑	❑	❑	❑
MATHEMATICS (I)—working with numbers and statistics; solving mathematical problems	❑	❑	❑	❑	❑	❑	❑	❑	❑	❑
MEDICAL SCIENCE (I)—studying or using the medical or biological sciences	❑	❑	❑	❑	❑	❑	❑	❑	❑	❑
MUSIC/DRAMATICS (A)—participating in the arts or watching others perform	❑	❑	❑	❑	❑	❑	❑	❑	❑	❑
ART (A)—creating or appreciating works of art	❑	❑	❑	❑	❑	❑	❑	❑	❑	❑
APPLIED ARTS (A)—creating or designing useful objects or art; doing crafts	❑	❑	❑	❑	❑	❑	❑	❑	❑	❑
WRITING (A)—reading, writing; enjoying language and literature	❑	❑	❑	❑	❑	❑	❑	❑	❑	❑
CULINARY ARTS (A)—cooking, entertaining; preparing and eating gourmet food	❑	❑	❑	❑	❑	❑	❑	❑	❑	❑

My Basic Interests

Basic Interest Area	Level of Interest					Level of Confidence in My Skills				
	5	4	3	2	1	5	4	3	2	1
TEACHING (S)—helping others learn; providing information and training	❑	❑	❑	❑	❑	❑	❑	❑	❑	❑
SOCIAL SERVICE (S)—serving others' needs; participating in group efforts	❑	❑	❑	❑	❑	❑	❑	❑	❑	❑
MEDICAL SERVICE (S)—caring for sick people; offering health services	❑	❑	❑	❑	❑	❑	❑	❑	❑	❑
RELIGIOUS ACTIVITIES (S)—participating in religion; ministering to others' spiritual needs	❑	❑	❑	❑	❑	❑	❑	❑	❑	❑
PUBLIC SPEAKING (E)—persuading people; making presentations	❑	❑	❑	❑	❑	❑	❑	❑	❑	❑
LAW/POLITICS (E)—debating, selling concepts; participating in politics	❑	❑	❑	❑	❑	❑	❑	❑	❑	❑
MERCHANDISING (E)—selling, buying, marketing	❑	❑	❑	❑	❑	❑	❑	❑	❑	❑
SALES (E)—influencing customers or potential customers; making a sale	❑	❑	❑	❑	❑	❑	❑	❑	❑	❑
ORGANIZATIONAL MANAGEMENT (E)—leading, organizing, motivating; taking charge of others	❑	❑	❑	❑	❑	❑	❑	❑	❑	❑
DATA MANAGEMENT (C)—compiling or organizing data; documenting	❑	❑	❑	❑	❑	❑	❑	❑	❑	❑
COMPUTER ACTIVITIES (C)—working with computers, software, or electronic equipment	❑	❑	❑	❑	❑	❑	❑	❑	❑	❑
OFFICE SERVICES (C)—performing clerical and administrative activities	❑	❑	❑	❑	❑	❑	❑	❑	❑	❑

Rating Your Confidence in Your Skills

The choices you make about what areas of interest to pursue may be influenced by a hidden variable: your beliefs about your ability to perform the tasks required in those areas of activity. If you don't think you're very good at something, you're not likely to pursue it, even if you have a strong interest in it. Conversely, if you know you're skilled in a certain area, you may think you should choose it even if your interest in it isn't strong.

It's very important, therefore, to be aware of how confident you are of your skills in each of the basic interest areas. If you know you lack confidence in an area in which you have strong interest, for example, you can more easily take steps to improve your confidence, rather than letting your fears convince you to avoid the area. Rating your level of skills confidence in each basic interest area is the purpose of the right-hand column in Worksheet 3. To complete this column, follow the instructions below.

Worksheet Directions

1. For each basic interest area in Worksheet 3, assess how much confidence you have in the skills and abilities you now possess in that area. Pay no attention to your interest ratings.

2. Rate your level of skills confidence using the following scale:

(Highest confidence)	5	I am very confident that I can perform these activities competently
	4	I believe I can perform most of the activities in this area reasonably well
	3	I have some doubts about my abilities in this area, but I believe I can perform at least some of the tasks
	2	I have little confidence in my skills in this area
(Lowest confidence)	1	I have no confidence in my skills in this area

A more formal evaluation of your skills confidence is available in the form of the *Skills Confidence Inventory,* an instrument designed to measure your skills confidence in each General Occupational Theme. This instrument can be completed in combination with the *Strong.*

Combining Confidence and Interest

Now that you have completed both parts of Worksheet 3, you are ready to consider your interests and your skills confidence levels at the same time.

If you scan your completed worksheet, you may notice that your level of interest in an area does not always match your level of skills confidence in that area. In fact, if you are like most people, your relationships to the basic interest areas fall into four different categories. There are areas in which you

- have both interest and confidence in your skills
- have interest but less skills confidence
- have little interest but substantial confidence in your skills
- have neither interest nor confidence

Obviously, these different categories call for different kinds of action. Basic interest areas in the first category are likely very important to you and deserve special consideration; those in the fourth are probably best avoided. Areas in which you have high interest but little confidence in your skills may represent areas of great potential for you; if you get training to improve your skills in these areas, you could open some new and exciting doors. Areas in which you have confidence in your skills but little interest may be areas you've explored in the past; these may or may not deserve some role in your new career or job. Worksheets 4 and 5 on pages 37 and 38 help you group the basic interest areas into these four categories.

Worksheet Directions

1. Find all the basic interest areas in Worksheet 3 (pages 33–34) that you marked 4 or 5 (if there are no areas marked 4 or 5, use areas marked 3). For each of these high-interest areas, look at your confidence rating. If your confidence rating is high (4 or 5), write the name of the interest area in Quadrant A on Worksheet 4. If your confidence rating is lower (3, 2, or 1), record the name of the interest area in Quadrant C.

2. Now find all the basic interest areas that you marked 3, 2, or 1. If the confidence rating of an area is high (4 or 5), write its name in Quadrant B; if its confidence rating is low (3, 2, or 1), write it in Quadrant D.

3. Now transfer the interest areas from each quadrant into Worksheet 5 on the next page. The completed table becomes an easy reference for possible action steps in your exploration of new and different paid work opportunities.

WORKSHEET 4. My Interests and Skills Confidence

Level of Interest

	HIGH	LOW
	[A]	[B]
HIGH		
LOW	[C]	[D]

Level of Skills Confidence

My Basic Interest Area Summary

Quadrant	What the Basic Interest Areas in This Quadrant Likely Mean to Me	Basic Interest Areas
A—strong interest and high skills confidence	These interest areas are important to me and need an outlet for expression, either on or off the job.	
B—weak interest but high skills confidence	These interest areas might be part of my work but should not be the central focus.	
C—strong interest but low skills confidence	These may be areas of untapped potential; I probably need training in them, but they could become central to my work.	
D—weak interest and low skills confidence	These are areas to avoid.	

Adding the Dimension of Personality Type

So far we've focused on discovering what you like to do as a way of finding more satisfying work options. Now we will approach this goal from the perspective of who you are.

Different jobs call on you to operate in different ways. Some jobs, for example, require a great deal of social contact—meeting new people, communicating face to face, working constantly with others. These jobs may not be the best choice for an Introvert, who usually prefers to work independently and to have quite a bit of time alone for reflection.

Fulfilling work calls on you to express your gifts. It lets you use your natural strengths and doesn't demand (too often) that you do things you don't like to do. When there is congruence—a good match—between you and your work, you will tend to be highly satisfied and energized. A mismatch between who you are and who the work demands you to be tends to cause stress and dissatisfaction.

Does your current job nourish your personality? Which aspects of your work reflect who you are and which do not? Exercise 4 will help you answer these important questions.

EXERCISE 4: Expressing Your Personality at Work

1. Write down all four of your preferences (the four components of your MBTI type; see Worksheet 2 on pages 25–26). For each, think about how your job calls upon you to express it. Are you able to express the preference most of the time, some of the time, or hardly ever?

2. Which of your four preferences is the most important for you to express in your work? You may or may not be able to express this gift as much as you would like. What kinds of activities are you involved in when you are playing to that gift? In these situations are you the only one with this gift or are you surrounded by others who share your preference? Write down these activities and describe the kinds of people with whom you are working at these times.

Now that you've evaluated your current work in terms of your preferences, its time to think about how you would ideally like to use your preferences in your work. Worksheet 6 allows you to do some systematic thinking about how your preferences need to find expression at work and how you may want to use the opposites of your preferences. Using your preferences will help you feel comfortable and at home; using their opposites (at the right times and in the right situations) will help your personal growth and allow you to develop balance.

Worksheet Directions

1. For each row of the chart in Worksheet 6, circle your preference (in the first column) and its opposite (in the third column).

2. Fill in the blank columns for that row, being as specific as possible. For example, if you are an Extravert, you might write in the "Use My Preference" column that you want to meet lots of new people and use your social and persuasive skills to convince them to buy a product, and you might write in the "Use My Opposite" column that you want a little time each day to work out marketing strategies and approaches on your own.

After identifying how you'd like to use your preferences at work, you can begin to identify specific positions or occupations that will allow you to use your preferences in these ways. For that process, we can provide only general guidance. MBTI types do not map directly to occupations. People of each MBTI type work in virtually every occupation. Knowing someone's type doesn't tell us everything about him or her. People with identical preferences will want to express those preferences differently.

Nevertheless, each MBTI type tends to prefer a certain kind of work environment. Table 4 on page 42 shows a few aspects of what each type desires regarding work activities. Locate your type and underline those elements that hold true for you.

WORKSHEET 6. My Preferences at Work

Preference	How I Would Like to Use My Preference at Work	Opposite of My Preference	How I Would Like to Use My Opposite at Work
E Extraversion or I Introversion		E Extraversion or I Introversion	
S Sensing or N Intuition		S Sensing or N Intuition	
T Thinking or F Feeling		T Thinking or F Feeling	
J Judging or P Perceiving		J Judging or P Perceiving	

Table 4. Important Characteristics of Work for Each MBTI Type

ISTJ	**ISFJ**	**INFJ**	**INTJ**
▪ Work behind the scenes ▪ Use skills in organizing and planning ▪ Enforce standards or maintain quality ▪ Influence others by providing clear direction	▪ Serve or help others rather than compete with them ▪ Use practical orientation ▪ Influence others in an under-stated way ▪ Be valued for attention to detail	▪ Work in solitude and with concentration ▪ Use creativity to help others ▪ Have a chance to implement dreams ▪ Share values and ideals with co-workers	▪ Use conceptual and analytical skills ▪ Have a chance to be the best ▪ Work autonomously on systemic problem solving ▪ Influence others by pushing them toward goals

ISTP	**ISFP**	**INFP**	**INTP**
▪ Troubleshoot and solve problems ▪ Work without much supervision ▪ Use project management skills ▪ Influence others by setting an example	▪ Express deeply held values ▪ Work in a supportive environ-ment ▪ Do practical work that benefits others ▪ Be independent but part of a team	▪ Have time for quiet and reflection ▪ Do work consistent with own values ▪ Rally others around a common purpose ▪ Work with little pressure	▪ Solve complex problems ▪ Influence others with logic ▪ Work with others who think independently ▪ Have quiet time for reflection

ESTP	**ESFP**	**ENFP**	**ENTP**
▪ Use negotiating skills to solve problems ▪ Influence others through humor and realism ▪ Create a fun-filled atmosphere ▪ Produce immediate results	▪ Pull people together in tense situations ▪ Facilitate efficient interactions ▪ Promote teamwork and high morale ▪ Be enthusiastic and positive	▪ Influence others with energy and enthusiasm ▪ Work in groups ▪ Support others with praise and encouragement ▪ Have variety and spontaneity	▪ Influence others through cleverness and expertise ▪ Design new ways of doing things ▪ Debate and interact with highly competent people

ESTJ	**ESFJ**	**ENFJ**	**ENTJ**
▪ Organize people and projects ▪ Influence others with decisiveness ▪ Create efficiency and stability ▪ Be part of an organization that values past experience	▪ Use skills in organizing and follow-through ▪ Give personal attention to others ▪ Work on teams ▪ Be part of an efficient and smooth-running organization	▪ Use ability to lead and facilitate ▪ Work harmoniously with others ▪ Influence others through participation ▪ Be part of an organizaiton with strong ideals	▪ Use ability to take charge ▪ Influence others by providing a vision ▪ Make steady progress toward goals ▪ Focus on tasks at hand

Source: Descriptions based in part on material from Hirsh and Kummerow, 1990.

Table 5 on page 44 provides another kind of information that you may find useful: a listing of some of the occupations people of each type commonly have. We have randomly selected just a few typical occupations for each type, as found in a variety of sources. We present this information not to tell you what you ought to be doing but to stimulate your thinking about what you might choose to do. Many occupation have the potential to fit your personality, depending on the specific circumstances of the particular position and the opportunities it gives you for expressing and further developing yourself.

As you think more about particular occupations and specific jobs, consider the kinds of people with whom you would most like to work. Do you want a setting in which you interact mostly with individuals who are somewhat like you or with a great variety of people? Are there certain types or kinds of type "cultures" in which you would prefer not to work? To address questions such as these in more detail, skip ahead to Chapter 5. There you will find exercises that will help you explore how you like to interact with others, how much structure you want in your work, and what values you want to express.

Putting It All Together: A Blueprint for Work-Life Transformation

Now that you have looked at your experiences, interests, skills, and personality in a systematic way, Worksheet 7 on pages 46–47 can help guide you in evaluating possible opportunities.

Worksheet Directions

Use the exercises you've completed in this chapter to give you ideas about each section in Worksheet 7. In some places you can transfer the results from a previous exercise directly into the blueprint. These are identified on page 47 and keyed by letter to the appropriate box.

Remember as you complete the blueprint that you aren't trying to finish the statement, "When I grow up I want to be a . . . ." Instead you are working toward

Table 5. Some Common Occupations of Each MBTI Type

ISTJ	ISFJ	INFJ	INTJ
Administrator	Social worker	Sociologist	Architect
Auditor	Librarian	Anthropologist	College professor
Accountant	Dental hygienist	Career counselor	Scientist
Engineer	Guidance counselor	Teacher	Physician
Realtor	Teacher	Artist	Financial planner
Technical writer	Interior decorator	Health care administrator	Computer programmer/Systems analyst

ISTP	ISFP	INFP	INTP
Craftsperson	Musician	Theologian	Systems analyst
Emergency medical technician	Sculptor	Therapist	Mathematician
Investment analyst	Art teacher	Writer	Computer programmer/Systems analyst
Forester	Visiting nurse	Social scientist	Information-graphics designer
Securities analyst	Medical assistant	Architect	Psychiatrist
Airline mechanic	Surveyor	Social worker	Financial planner

ESTP	ESFP	ENFP	ENTP
Pilot	Salesperson	Elementary schoolteacher	Consultant
Physical therapist	Customer service representative	Guidance counselor	Marketing professional
Purchasing agent	Medical assistant	Journalist	Advertising creative director
Investments manager	Occupational therapist	Public relations specialist	Journalist
Realtor	Travel agent	Physical therapist	Realtor
Insurance investigator	Team trainer	Management consultant	Art director

ESTJ	ESFJ	ENFJ	ENTJ
Operations manager	Nurse	Author	Business executive
Athletic coach	Speech pathologist	Trainer	Military officer
Insurance agent	Teacher	Psychologist	Investment banker
Paralegal	Paralegal	Outplacement consultant	Management trainer
Credit analyst	Credit counselor	Occupational therapist	Lawyer
Technical trainer	Social worker	Social worker	Administrator

finishing the statement, "My next paid work opportunity needs to have the following elements: . . . ."

This blueprint will help you explore and evaluate options that exist. Use it as an aid for judging whether a particular opportunity really matches you. Suppose you have heard of work that sounds appealing on the surface. Pick up the blueprint and use it to help you figure out whether the appeal goes beyond the superficial. Or you can use the blueprint as a discussion tool. Sit down with a friend and talk about what you have written. Ask the friend to help you brainstorm the kinds of work activities, positions, or organizations that would be most likely to fit with who you are.

In Chapter 10 we deal with the entire process of reinventing yourself, helping you know where to go from here. You can turn to that chapter now if you like. If you are truly ready to mobilize resources and move right into a job-search process, look at Appendix B for a listing of useful resources.

WORKSHEET 7. A Blueprint for Finding My Ideal Job

A. Most appealing kinds of work settings	B. Kinds of people with whom I like to work
C. Interests I would like to express at work	D. Skills I would like to use at work
E. Activities or tasks I would like to avoid	F. How much interaction I want with others

G. Gifts (preferences) I most need to express	H. A new skill or interest I'd like to explore
I. Occupations that sound appealing	J. An area of untapped potential for me

You will find it helpful to refer to the following worksheets and exercises:

A. Look at the descriptions of the General Occupational Themes in Worksheet 1 (pp. 16-17) or Table 1 (p. 12) for ideas.

C. See Worksheet 3, "My Basic Interests," pp. 33-34.

D. Look at the descriptions of the General Occupational Themes in Worksheet 1 (pp. 16-17) or Table 1 (p. 12) for ideas.

E. See Worksheet 3, "My Basic Interests," pp. 33-34.

G. See Exercise 4, "Expressing Your Personality at Work," p. 39.

H. See Exercises 1, 2, and 3, p. 29.

J. See Worksheet 5, "My Basic Interest Area Summary," p. 38.

5

TRANSFORMING YOUR WORK LIFE— VOLUNTEER WORK

Volunteer work can be highly rewarding. It gives you a chance to apply your skills, learn new skills, try out a new kind of work—all while helping those in need or advancing a cause in which you believe. Volunteering may play an important role in reinventing the work circle of your life if you

- no longer have to spend the bulk of your time generating income but still feel a need to do more than sit around and relax
- have more extra time and want to be more actively involved in your community or express an area of interest different from your paid work
- want to explore new paid-work options or build up the necessary skills for doing so

Volunteer opportunities are numerous and varied. They can involve any kind of work activity you can imagine, any level of time commitment you wish, and any degree of responsibility.

The chances are that your work to date has reflected many of your interests, or else you would not have continued doing it for an extended period of time. But you may have additional interests that you have not satisfied, or your old job may have parts that you would just as soon not replace. This can be a time to pause in your life and ask yourself, What do I truly enjoy doing? What really matters to me? and What will I choose to do now that the choice is more clearly mine? Volunteering can help you answer these questions; the right volunteer work may even be the answer itself!

Finding a rewarding and satisfying volunteer position is much like finding the ideal job, and the *Strong Interest Inventory* and the *Myers-Briggs Type Indicator* can assist you in this process in a similar way. But there is one major difference: The typical volunteer role is not as clearly or rigidly defined as the typical paid work position. There may be no formal job title or job description. The advantage in this is that you are likely to have a great deal of latitude in defining your role as a volunteer.

Why Volunteer?

Many people don't consider the possibility of doing volunteer work because of beliefs they have about the nature of the experience. Many of these beliefs, however, turn out to be unfounded. If a part of you is resisting the idea of volunteering, consider the following:

Volunteering can bring financial rewards.

By definition, volunteer activities do not provide large financial compensation for your time and efforts. But volunteering doesn't always mean working for free, and it needn't cost you any money. Many volunteer activities provide compensation for direct expenses you incur. If you are faced with out-of-pocket costs in the course of volunteering, some of those costs, such as those for transportation, may be deductible from your taxes. Other expenses may be reimbursed by the volunteer agency for which you work. Volunteer opportunities may even have additional financial benefits, such as token compensation, meals, memberships, or the opportunity to use facilities for which you would otherwise be charged. In addition, the skills you learn while volunteering may translate into paid work later on.

Volunteer positions are typically flexible enough to allow you plenty of time to do other things.

Many volunteer activities require only a part-time commitment, whether on a regular schedule or on a flexible schedule that might reflect your changing needs. And some volunteers work only periodically. You can give your volunteer work a portion of your time and energy and still have plenty left for pursuing your hobbies, traveling, working at a paid job, or spending time with friends and family.

Volunteer work helps you prepare for the transition to retirement.

One of the most difficult transitions a person faces in his or her work life is to retire from a lifelong career and then have no idea of what to do next. Part-time volunteering can provide you with the opportunity to explore your interests and values before you retire and to identify or construct the kind of volunteer experience that will fill (perhaps even more satisfactorily) the role that paid work now plays in your life.

Volunteer work can bring you respect and prestige.

The size of your salary is not the only thing that can generate respect and bring admiration from others. Respect can come from the skillful application of knowledge, from making a contribution that has a positive impact on someone else's life, from living according to a principle or value, from making an organization run more smoothly, or from taking the time to try to make things around you just a little bit better. Many volunteer activities allow you the opportunity to gain the respect of others in these ways; some are very much in the public eye.

**Volunteers can wield considerable power
and be involved in high-level decision making.**

The tasks that volunteers take on are often the tasks that
others can't afford to pay individuals to perform—but
this reality doesn't mean that the tasks aren't important.
Some volunteers do work that involves substantial
responsibility and power. For example, retired executives
work with SCORE (Service Corps of Retired Executives)
as consultants to businesses, helping the owners better
manage and develop their businesses. Former President
Jimmy Carter works with Habitat for Humanity, helping
to build houses for people who cannot afford to pay for
the work. In the political realm, volunteers play key roles
that often enable them to exert considerable influence.

**Volunteering allows you to meet and work
with new and interesting people.**

If you seek volunteer work, you're likely to meet a great
variety of new people. You can make new acquaintances,
some of whom may become new friends who will share
your dreams and dilemmas over the next part of your life.
Volunteering can be an excellent way to meet one of the
constant challenges of aging—to maintain and replenish
a base of friends and colleagues as old friends move away,
become infirm, or die.

**Volunteering can be an opportunity to do
something new and different.**

One of the most exciting aspects of volunteering is that it
provides an opportunity for you to try something new.
Most organizations that want volunteers aren't picky about
specific qualifications or experience. You can often begin
working in a position with only some necessary foundation
skills—the rest you can learn as you go. If you are looking
for real change, explore types of volunteer positions that
are very different from what you have been doing.

Finding the Ideal
Volunteer Position

Volunteer positions, like jobs, are made up of different activities and exist in a variety of environments. Your task is going to be to tease out the activities that are of interest to you, then to identify volunteer environments that will allow you to perform those preferred activities and provide you with opportunities to pursue your interests and preferences. The exercises that follow are designed to help you with this process; what they help you discover about yourself may be applied to identifying suitable volunteer opportunities as well as the types of paid work that suit you best.

What Can I Do That Will Be
Appreciated by Others?

If making a contribution is important to you, think about agencies that can use the skills and knowledge that you have accumulated over the years. Many things you know about and can do may be very much appreciated by others, even if you take them for granted.

Worksheet 8 on page 54 can help you identify your areas of skill and knowledge that are of potential value in volunteer work. It groups activities into the six General Occupational Themes of the *Strong,* which are explained in Chapter 2.

Worksheet Directions

> In the center column of Worksheet 8, mark areas in which you have experience or skill; in the right-hand column, write in any similar or related skills you have that others might recognize and value.

What Activities Do I Want
to Be Involved In?

The Basic Interest Scales on the *Strong* offer a fairly detailed, precise look at the activities that interest you. If you have a

WORKSHEET 8. What I Have to Offer

General Occupational Themes	My Skills and Abilities	Other Related Skills and Abilities
Realistic	❑ I can work skillfully with my hands ❑ I know how to work with specialized tools or machines ❑ I can fix things that others do not seem to understand	
Investigative	❑ I can do research ❑ I can help others understand and solve problems ❑ I can help others learn how to learn ❑ I can explain complex concepts in simple terms	
Artistic	❑ I can create things that are pleasing to the senses ❑ I can match colors, arrange objects ❑ I can make music ❑ I can write clearly	
Social	❑ I can communicate with and gain the trust of others ❑ I can recognize and minister to others' needs ❑ I can teach or coach others	
Enterprising	❑ I can clearly define organizational goals ❑ I can persuade others to pursue organizational goals ❑ I can motivate people to work together ❑ I can sell products, ideas, or programs	
Conventional	❑ I can organize data and information ❑ I can make order out of chaos ❑ I can accomplish tasks in an orderly fashion	

high level of interest in the Realistic Theme, for example, the Basic Interest Scales tell you if your Realistic interests are oriented toward working with mechanical devices and machinery or toward being involved with nature.

If you have worked through Chapter 4 or taken the *Strong,* you have already identified the basic interest areas in which you have the highest interest. Turn back to pages 33–34 and review Worksheet 3. Which areas of greatest interest do you want to express in a volunteer position?

Also review Worksheets 4 and 5 on pages 37 and 38. Are there any areas in which you have high interest but not much confidence in your skills? You may want to focus on some of these areas in your volunteer work as a way of increasing your confidence in your skills.

If you have neither taken the *Strong* nor worked through Chapter 4, we recommend you complete the three worksheets in Chapter 4 mentioned above. They will help you focus your search for rewarding volunteer work.

How Much People Interaction Do I Want?

This question is basic to finding your ideal work—whether volunteer or paid. The social aspect of volunteering might be what you would enjoy most. If so, choosing a volunteer activity that involves frequent interaction with others will be important. If you prefer less contact with people, you may want to consider volunteer activities that focus more on using mechanical skills or accumulating and using information. Worksheet 9 on page 57 can help you determine your preference for social interaction.

If you are not very clear about the level of social interaction you want in your volunteer work, both the MBTI and the *Strong* can tell you about how, when, and how much you like to interact with others. For example, if you have strong interest in the Social and/or Enterprising Themes, you likely enjoy activities in which people are central to your work. Conversely, strong interest in the Investigative and/or Realistic Themes suggests you prefer working more with things, ideas, or data. MBTI preferences in the Introversion—Extraversion dimension correspond with these patterns as well: Extraverts prefer lots of people contact, and Introverts, needing time alone for reflection, prefer the more limited people contact involved in working with things, ideas, or data.

Worksheet Directions

Work through Worksheet 9 to determine your orientation to social interaction. Check a box in the second row only if you've taken the *Strong* (the Work Style scale is one of the Personal Style Scales on the last page of the Profile).

The orientation people have to social interaction is a continuum. You can clearly prefer one pole or the other, or you can have mixed preferences. For example, you may have strong interest in both the Realistic and Investigative Themes, yet be an Extravert. Or your two areas of greatest interest may be Social and Investigative, each suggesting a different orientation to social contact. If such patterns appeared when you completed Worksheet 9, the information that follows may help you understand your mixed orientation to people interaction.

An interest in working with ideas, data, or things does not necessarily mean that you are not skilled or comfortable working with people. Similarly, an interest in working with people does not mean that you are not skilled in working with data or with things. You could, for example, love to teach about technical subjects (reflecting an ability to work with things, ideas, and data) in a way that allows you to work closely with others (reflecting an interest in working with people).

It is also important to understand that the dichotomy Extraversion—Introversion is different from interests because it is based on the kind of activity (outwardly or inwardly focused) that generates energy for you. Typically, if you are working at the opposite end of the dichotomy from your

WORKSHEET 9. My Preferred Type of Social Interaction

	A	B
My interests are strongest in:	❏ the Enterprising and Social Themes	❏ the Realistic and Investigative Themes
On the *Strong's* Work Style scale, I scored toward:	❏ the People pole	❏ the Ideas/Data/Things pole
I have a preference for:	❏ Extraversion	❏ Introversion

Unique ways in which I prefer to interact with others and meet my social needs

If you marked items in column A only, you
- like frequent contact with others
- like to be part of large groups and work through problems in a group
- spend a lot of time talking about things

If you marked items in column B only, you
- prefer to work alone and independently
- likely have a few close friends
- do not spend much time talking about ideas until they are complete

If you marked items in both columns, you have mixed or complex preferences in the area of social interaction.

preference, you will find yourself tiring, and you will feel a need to operate at the preferred end of the dichotomy to get recharged. An interest in a people-oriented Theme (e.g., Social) combined with a preference for Introversion may mean that you would like to work with people or on people-related issues but in a way that leaves you time for reflection. Similarly, an interest in a things-oriented Theme (e.g., Realistic) combined with a preference for Extraversion suggests that you would like to work with things in a way that allows you lots of social interaction.

With Whom Do I Want to Associate?

The kinds of people you work with in your volunteer position can make the difference between a rewarding experience and a frustrating one. Many people find that they are most comfortable working with others who have similar interests. You can begin and maintain conversations with them more easily. If you're a Conventional type, for example, you might like being around other Conventional types but feel like a fish out of water associating with mostly Artistic types. On the other hand, some people like working with others who have interests different from theirs. People with different interests can teach you new things and give you a richer social experience.

If you think you'll prefer being around people who mostly share your interests, it can be helpful to do some systematic thinking about who is likely to have interests similar to yours, and in what organizations, positions, and environments you're likely to find them. The Occupational Scales on the *Strong* can assist you with this process. The scales are scored by comparing your likes and dislikes with those of people satisfactorily employed in a wide variety of occupations. Therefore, if you score high on a particular Occupational Scale, your interests are likely to be very similar to people in that occupation. Worksheet 10 on page 60 allows you to summarize and apply this information from the *Strong* Profile.

Worksheet Directions

If you have taken the *Strong,* look at the Occupational Scales section of the Snapshot and find the occupations for which you have a score of "Similar" or "Very Similar." Write these in the left column of Worksheet 10. If no occupations with a score of "Similar" or higher appear on your Snapshot, turn to pages 3–5 of your Profile and find the Occupational Scales with scores of 35 or higher. If you haven't taken the *Strong,* complete this part of the worksheet based on your experience and self-knowledge.

Next, for each occupation you've listed, think of volunteer activities in which people in that occupation—or people with the same kind of interests—are likely to be involved, and list these in the center column. For example, if you have a high score on "Social worker" on the *Strong* Profile and list this occupation in the left column, you could list "adult literacy training" or "homeless shelter work" in the center column.

Last, you may want to fill in the right column because it is often possible to identify volunteer opportunities that might be fun and rewarding by talking with people who share your interests. Ask these friends and acquaintances about the volunteer activities in which they are involved or would like to be involved, and add these activities to the middle column of the worksheet.

How Much Structure Do I Want in My Volunteer Work?

Some volunteer positions are quite structured, involving set routines and well-defined activities and responsibilities. Others are more open-ended, with changing demands and requirements and little routine or repetitious work. In which type of position would you be most comfortable and happy?

WORKSHEET 10. Volunteer Work with People Who Share My Interests

Occupations of People Who Share My Interests	Volunteer Activities Involving Contact with Such People	Individuals I Know in These Occupations

Your results on the *Strong* (or the Theme code you developed in Worksheet 1, pages 16–17) can help you answer this question. The Conventional Theme captures an interest in structure, predictability, careful attention to detail, and comfort with rules and the routine. The Artistic Theme, concerned by definition with interests in the sensual and esthetic, captures an interest in the new and different, and the possibilities that lie in novel situations. The creative, by definition a breaking of the rules, is in many ways the opposite of the Conventional. Therefore, if the Artistic Theme is part of your Theme code, you are likely to prefer positions that allow spontaneity and flexibility; if the Conventional Theme is in your Theme code, you probably are most comfortable with a more structured position. If you are one of the rare individuals who has strong interests in both Themes, your relationship to structure in your work is harder to determine, as it is if your main interests lie in any of the other four themes.

Your MBTI preferences offer insight into this issue also. Sensing and Judging preferences together capture much of the Conventional Theme, reflecting a logical and organized approach to dealing with the tangible, quantifiable information available in the present moment. People with this combination of preferences tend to get immersed in the immediate task and seek to systematically piece together information according to some system or set of guidelines. Intuition and Perceiving preferences together, in contrast, have a close relationship to the Artistic Theme, reflecting a much less structured, more flexible, future-oriented approach, one with a looser connection to immediate, tangible concerns. People with Intuition and Judging preferences, or Sensing and Perceiving preferences, fall somewhere in the middle between these two ends of the continuum.

Figure 3 on page 62 summarizes the relationships among interests, preferences, and the orientation toward structure and the lack of structure. If you don't remember your preferences, look back at Worksheet 2, pages 25–26, to review your preference for Sensing vs. Intuition and Judging vs. Perceiving. Where do you fall in the spectrum illustrated in Figure 3? If you

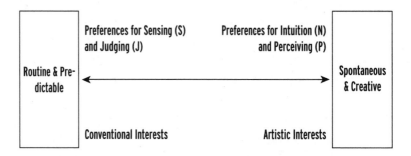

FIGURE 3. Structured vs. Unstructured Work

have a strong orientation toward one end or the other, you may
need a matching volunteer experience in order to feel fulfilled.

What Kind of Work Environment Do I Want?
Work environments are defined by the type of organization,
the organization's goal or mission, the culture of the organization, and the types of people who make up the organization. It
is important for the environment in which you volunteer to
match your interests and personal style.

If you have read Chapter 2, you may recall that each General Occupational Theme is associated with a set of work environments. These environments are those in which people with
interests in that Theme typically work. A look at the work environments connected with the General Occupational Themes in
your Theme code may help you locate environments that you
will enjoy. You can use Worksheet 11 to find suitable environments and Worksheet 12 on page 65 to summarize what you
learn about your work environment preferences.

Worksheet Directions

1. Go through Worksheet 11 with a highlighter or pencil and
mark those environments that have some appeal for you,
paying particular attention to the Themes in your Theme
code. Then go through the chart again, this time crossing
out those environments that have no appeal. Consider what
you have enjoyed and not enjoyed in the past, as well as
what you predict you would enjoy or not enjoy.

WORKSHEET 11. My Preferred Work Environments

Realistic	Social
■ Outdoor environments ■ Environments in which there is minimal interaction with others ■ Organizations with casual dress ■ Organizations with clearly drawn lines of authority ■ Organizations with tangible products ■ Action-oriented organizations	■ Social service agencies, schools, religious organizations ■ Personnel offices ■ Health care facilities and clinics ■ Environments in which people talk things over

Investigative	Enterprising
■ Unstructured organizations that allow freedom in workstyles ■ Achievement-oriented institutions ■ Research and development labs, colleges, medical facilities; computer-related environments ■ Environments that stress consideration of alternatives rather than action or decision	■ Seats of power; political organizations, financial institutions ■ Manufacturing and sales firms ■ Fund-raising organizations ■ Small, independently owned businesses ■ Environments that stress quick and confident action with little discussion

Artistic	Conventional
■ Unstructured, flexible organizations that allow self-expression ■ Institutions that teach artistic skills ■ Artistic studios, theaters, concert halls ■ Museums, libraries, galleries ■ Environments in which no one tells you what to do	■ Large, structured organizations with well-ordered chains of command ■ Business, financial, and accounting institutions ■ Quality-control and inspection departments ■ Environments in which others tell you what to do

2. After you have completed Worksheet 11, use Worksheet 12 to describe more fully the environments in which you would like to work and in which you could not work. In the left-hand column, write in the most appealing environments you highlighted in Worksheet 11. Add any work environments you've actually experienced that aren't listed on the worksheet. Also write down the characteristics of the environments that make them attractive or enjoyable. In the right-hand column, list the environments you crossed out on Worksheet 11, and add any others with which you have had undesirable experiences that aren't listed in the worksheet.

What Kind of Volunteer Work Is Most Consistent with My Values?

What do you want out of your volunteer experience? What motivates you to donate your time to an organization? Much of the answer to these questions will come not from your interests but from your values. Values are different from interests. Interests are an indication of what you like to do, whereas values are an indication of what is important to you. We refer to our values when we make choices.

Values often become more important during the latter half of one's life. You may have a long list of accomplishments but still have a feeling that you haven't yet done what's really important. You may want to ask yourself, What do I still want to accomplish in my life that's consistent with my values?

Both your *Strong* results and your MBTI preferences can offer you information about your values. Worksheet 13 on page 67 lists some of the key values typically associated with interests in each of the General Occupational Themes as well as values associated with each of four MBTI preference combinations.

WORKSHEET 12. Work Environments for Me to Consider and to Avoid

Most Attractive Work Environments	Least Attractive Work Environments

Worksheet Directions

Use your marker to highlight in Worksheet 13 those values that are important to you. Don't worry about what you should" value; instead try to identify what you truly value. Your most important values are likely to be those associated with your strongest interests and your preferences, but some important values may lie in other areas too.

After you have identified your values, try to link them to the specific work environments and volunteer activities you've identified in Worksheets 10, 11, and 12. When you consider various volunteer opportunities, evaluate how well each will match your values.

What's Next?

We hope that your work in this chapter has helped you understand the nature of volunteering and clarify what it is you are looking for in a volunteer experience. If so, your next task is to locate volunteer opportunities and take a closer look at them. You can use a variety of strategies, from looking in your local newspaper for organizations that are seeking volunteers to asking your friends what they are doing. In Appendix B, we have listed resources that may help you to locate appropriate opportunities. At this point we would like to reassure you that a successful search is more likely when you know what you are looking for.

My Most Important Values

Values Associated with the General Occupational Themes

Realistic	Social
■ Practicality, thrift	■ Idealism, ethical behavior
■ Persistence	■ Responsibility
■ Modesty	■ Cooperation, generosity
■ Tradition	■ Concern for the welfare of others

Investigative	Enterprising
■ Independence, curiosity	■ Status
■ Objective analysis	■ Ambition, competition
■ Creativity	■ Optimism
■ Truth	■ Power, material possessions

Artistic	Conventional
■ Independence, nonconformity	■ Conscientiousness
■ Self-expression	■ Order
■ Sensitivity, emotion	■ Precision and accuracy
■ Beauty	■ Money, material possessions

Values Associated with MBTI Preference Combinations

Sensing-Thinking (ST)	Intuition-Thinking (NT)
■ Practicality, matter-of-fact style	■ Logic and ingenuity
■ Impersonal analysis of concrete facts	■ Impersonal analysis of possibilities
■ Step-by-step logical thinking	■ Theoretical and technical developments

Sensing-Feeling (SF)	Intuition-Feeling (NF)
■ Sympathy and friendliness	■ Enthusiasm and insight
■ Warmth and subjective decision making	■ Patterns, symbolic meaning, theoretical relationships
■ Facts about people	■ Unfolding of possibilities, especially for people

Source: Based in part on Harmon, Hansen, Borgen, and Hammer, 1994.

6

REDISCOVERING LEARNING

Learning continues throughout your life. You would be hard pressed to find someone who would argue with that statement. Nevertheless, many people over the age of 50 hesitate when asked, "How about taking a class?" Perhaps you have had that hesitation yourself. You would be the oldest in the class. You wonder if your study habits are too rusty, and you feel intimidated by the thought of taking a test.

Many people do shy away from formal learning after the age of 30 or 40 because of the societal expectation that formal learning should be over by then. By age 30 or 40 a person already has a career. You may still learn on the job, but going back to school is like . . . taking a step backwards.

Despite such attitudes, reality is quite a bit different. Adults of all ages are engaging in formal education like never before, giving greater attention to the circle of learning in their lives. The average age of college students has been rising steadily; in 1997 it stood at 36 years old. This statistic reflects the fact that a great many college students are in their 40s, 50s, and 60s, balancing out the proportion that are 18 to 22. In fact, 50 percent of all college students today are older than 25. That means you will hardly be an anomaly if you go "back" to school. Just drop in to a continuing education or adult education program office at your local community college and see for yourself how adult learners are being courted and catered to.

In short, if you have been daydreaming about finishing a degree, entering a new field that requires formal training, or just immersing yourself in a learning environment, there's nothing to stop you!

We hope you use this chapter as a catalyst for exploring learning opportunities. No matter what purpose you have in mind for learning (from skills training to learning for fun), this chapter can be a helpful guide. While you work through the exercises and activities that follow, suspend any beliefs you have that tell you education is not an option. Let yourself really look at what role you want learning to play in your life.

Why Do I Want to Learn?

If you're like most people, your earlier formal education was a mixed bag. You had inspiring teachers and not-so-inspiring ones, times when learning was great fun and times when you couldn't bear to be in school. Exercise 5 is designed to jog your memory and get you back in touch with your positive learning experiences.

EXERCISE 5: Getting in Touch with a Favored Memory of School

The distant past can speak volumes to you about what you might wish to experience again. Ask someone to read the passage below to you while you close your eyes and relax, or read the passage to yourself and then close the book so you can bring the memory vividly back to life. Give yourself psychological space to relive the experience.

Picture yourself back in school in a class you really enjoyed. See yourself again as the learner. Notice who is there. Pay attention to what you are doing. Notice what others are doing. Hear again what is being said and the sounds that are around you. Absorb the smells once again. See yourself moving through time in that class. Feel again what you felt then. Enjoy the memory. When you are ready, open your eyes.

When you are finished, write down a few key words or phrases to remind you of what you experienced. You will be using information from this exercise later when we explore what your MBTI preferences suggest about your orientation to learning.

WORKSHEET 14. Why Do I Want to Learn?

In rank order, my goals for learning are:

_____ to acquire a skill I can apply in my current job

_____ to build an entirely new area of expertise or knowledge for a new career

_____ to satisfy my intellectual curiosity and desire to learn

_____ to pursue a hobby or interest I have always admired from afar

_____ to keep myself mentally alert and involved in the world around me

_____ to relearn a dormant skill I loved in my younger days

_____ to meet others who are interested in similar things

_____ to have fun

_____ to gain a sense of achievement or mastery

_____ to be able to earn more money

Now that you have toyed with memories, it's time to day-dream. Your pictures of yourself in the future can be as vivid as your recollections. Take a few moments to think about yourself in the future as a learner. You might even imagine yourself in that future learning situation you have always thought would be ideal. What would really draw you toward learning? What is on your wish list?

After you've given yourself time to daydream about learning, look at Worksheet 14.

Worksheet Directions

Worksheet 14 shows a list of 10 common reasons people have for pursuing further learning. Rank these reasons for your future, assigning a 1 to your most important reason and a 10 to your least important reason. This process will help you articulate and crystallize what you want from learning experiences in your life.

Assuming you want to focus on the second circle of life through some kind of formal learning, you need to answer two main questions for yourself: What exactly do I want to learn? How would I like to learn it? To begin to answer the first question, you'll do an activity based on the framework of the *Strong*. To answer the second, you'll work through a set of activities based on both the *Strong* and the MBTI that help you determine your preferred learning style.

What Do I Want to Learn?

The answer to this question depends, of course, on your reason for wanting to learn. What reasons did you rate #1 and #2 in Worksheet 14 on the previous page? If learning itself is your primary goal, you can be guided by interest alone. You can choose skills and areas of knowledge you are itching to learn or to master; the main issue will be deciding which areas are most intriguing or important to you. If your goal is training for a new career or job, interest is still important, but you may have a particular skill or knowledge gap that you need to close.

In either case, the General Occupational Themes on the *Strong* (R, I, A, S, E, C) provide an excellent framework for beginning the process of choosing and prioritizing areas of learning. Recall your Theme code (on the Snapshot page of your *Strong* Profile if you have taken the *Strong;* the one that emerged from Worksheet 1, pages 16 – 17, if you haven't). The themes in your personal Theme code are all areas of real interest for you. Each relates to a broad band of potential learning activities.

Worksheet 15 on pages 74 – 75 allows you to use the General Occupational Themes in your Theme code to target more specific subject areas that relate directly to educational programs, majors, and classes.

Worksheet Directions

1. Find the Theme in Worksheet 15 in which you have the highest interest. Mark the subject areas within the Theme you want to learn and those you need to learn in order to fill a knowledge or skill gap (some subject areas may be both).

Don't worry about whether you have talent in an area—
just focus on your attraction to the subject or its role in
reaching a specific goal.

2. On the blank lines provided, add any subject areas related
to this Theme that you have considered learning more
about or need to learn.

3. Repeat this process with the other Themes in your
Theme code, and then with all the remaining Themes. You
may need to learn skills or knowledge in an area in which
you have little interest in order to reach a goal, or you may
be interested in a specific subject that connects to a Theme
in which you have only moderate or little interest.

Now you have a set of possibilities. You may want to use a separate sheet of paper to list the items you've marked on Worksheet
15 in order of priority, thinking about both what would be most
enjoyable as well as most useful. If you have a specific goal in
mind, consider how each subject area relates to that goal.

The next step is to find out where you can learn the subjects or skills you've identified. You may know of educational
resources available to you in your community where you can
begin learning your chosen subjects. But for some subject areas
you may need to investigate providers.

Before you jump into the investigation process, however,
there is another factor to consider. How you like to learn can be
as critical as the content itself.

How Do I Like to Learn?

People have different learning styles. Some people like hands-
on learning, others like concepts and lectures. Some prefer
learning alone at their own pace, while others excel in a group
environment. Think back to Exercise 5 on page 70. How were
you learning when the experience was a positive one? What was
the environment like? Were you involved with others? If so, in
what way?

Subjects on Which I Can Focus

Subject Areas	Want to Learn	Need to Learn
Realistic		
Gardening, caring for plants	❏	❏
Taking care of animals	❏	❏
Animal medicine	❏	❏
Bird-watching	❏	❏
Construction	❏	❏
Remodeling or building	❏	❏
Fixing or remodeling cars	❏	❏
Playing a certain sport	❏	❏
Repairing equipment	❏	❏
Emergency medicine	❏	❏
_____	❏	❏
_____	❏	❏
Investigative		
The physical environment	❏	❏
Mathematics	❏	❏
Playing chess or bridge	❏	❏
Natural sciences	❏	❏
Creative problem solving	❏	❏
Health or wellness	❏	❏
Conducting research	❏	❏
Statistics	❏	❏
Psychology	❏	❏
_____	❏	❏
_____	❏	❏
Artistic		
Singing or playing an instrument	❏	❏
Acting	❏	❏
Sculpture	❏	❏
Drawing or painting	❏	❏
Creative writing	❏	❏
Gourmet or ethnic cooking	❏	❏
Entertaining	❏	❏
Speaking another language	❏	❏
Newsletter writing	❏	❏
Graphic design	❏	❏
_____	❏	❏
_____	❏	❏

Subject Areas	Want to Learn	Need to Learn
Social		
Counseling	☐	☐
Group facilitation	☐	☐
Teaching	☐	☐
Customer service	☐	☐
Religion	☐	☐
Coaching	☐	☐
Caring for children	☐	☐
Team skills	☐	☐
Human rights	☐	☐
_____	☐	☐
_____	☐	☐
Enterprising		
Selling	☐	☐
Public speaking	☐	☐
Negotiating	☐	☐
Managing people	☐	☐
Creating business plans	☐	☐
Politics	☐	☐
Running a campaign	☐	☐
Public relations	☐	☐
_____	☐	☐
_____	☐	☐
Conventional		
Computer programming	☐	☐
Basic computer skills	☐	☐
Use of software packages	☐	☐
Accounting	☐	☐
Finance skills	☐	☐
Time management	☐	☐
Project management	☐	☐
Word processing	☐	☐
Desktop publishing	☐	☐
Stock market knowledge	☐	☐
_____	☐	☐
_____	☐	☐

Knowing how you like to learn is important because there are numerous avenues for learning, some traditional and some not. In addition to the traditional college programs based on lectures and book-learning, you can choose from experientially oriented vocational programs, internships and externships, apprenticeships, educational tours and work trips, adventure trips, and so on. In many content areas you really do have a choice of how to learn.

The type or style of learning that most appeals to you has a great deal to do with your MBTI preferences. Here in general are what the dichotomies of the MBTI will help you focus on:

Extraversion vs. Introversion

How much do I want to interact with others in my learning?

Sensing vs. Intuition

What kind of balance do I want between theory and practice?

Thinking vs. Feeling

What's most important for me, challenge or support?

Judging vs. Perceiving

How much structure do I prefer?

Worksheet 16 on pages 77–78 will help you translate your preferences into a preferred learning style.

Worksheet Directions

Considering one dichotomy at a time, circle every item on Worksheet 16 that you enjoy or that appeals to you. Don't limit yourself to the items listed under your preferences. Also, the items are not paired as opposites, so don't worry if you want to mark items directly across from each other.

Components of My Learning Style in Relation to My MBTI Preferences

Extraversion	Introversion
<ul><li>Learning in groups</li><li>Talking about what I am learning</li><li>Learning about a variety of topics</li><li>Discussing topics with a partner</li><li>Participating in interactive learning tasks</li><li>Making presentations</li><li>Being expected to be verbal in class</li></ul>	<ul><li>Reading about a topic</li><li>Having time to prepare before I am called on</li><li>Doing self-directed study projects</li><li>Using software for learning</li><li>Learning through a correspondence program</li><li>Having individualized learning goals</li><li>Being tutored one-on-one</li></ul>
Sensing	Intuition
<ul><li>Seeing skills demonstrated</li><li>Doing hands-on activities</li><li>Reading how-to books</li><li>Building tangible things</li><li>Learning from an expert</li><li>Using a proven system</li><li>Having specific training activities</li><li>Participating in short-term programs</li><li>Learning facts and history</li></ul>	<ul><li>Learning about theory</li><li>Having opportunities to brainstorm</li><li>Learning about concepts</li><li>Figuring out patterns and meanings on my own</li><li>Doing imaginative activities</li><li>Listening to thought-provoking lectures</li><li>Taking part in intellectual discussions</li><li>Learning in an academic setting</li></ul>

Thinking	Feeling
■ Engaging in debates with others ■ Participating in a nationally recognized program ■ Learning from someone I respect ■ Being able to measure myself and my progress ■ Fine-tuning a personal competency ■ Working with competent participants ■ Being challenged and given tough feedback	■ Getting frequent feedback ■ Learning from someone I like ■ Learning in a nongraded and nonevaluative environment ■ Helping others learn ■ Having a mentor ■ Working with caring participants ■ Getting individualized, supportive attention ■ Being myself; not having to play a role

Judging	Perceiving
■ Having a set structure and agenda ■ Working from a set of goals ■ Following a systematic process ■ Being encouraged to set personal objectives ■ Having a well-organized instructor ■ Having time to prepare ■ Being disciplined to finish assignments ■ Feeling that I have worked hard	■ Creating the learning activities as I go ■ Learning in an unstructured environment ■ Having several options ■ Learning from a spontaneous, creative instructor ■ Experimenting with different techniques ■ Having the freedom to design my own learning ■ Having fun while learning

Now that you have identified some aspects of your learning style, consider your style as a whole. What patterns do you see on the worksheet? Are your preferred modes of learning predicted by your MBTI type? Are there any aspects of your learning style that have been limiting you in any way? How can you use what you know about your learning style to realize the goals you identified in Worksheet 14? Do you want to push yourself to experiment with types of learning with which you aren't entirely comfortable?

Your results on the *Strong* can also tell you about your learning style. If you've taken the *Strong,* turn to the Personal Style Scales on the last page of your Profile. Three scales there relate to how you like to learn: the Work Style scale, the Learning Environment scale, and the Risk Taking/Adventure scale. The Work Style scale has some similarity to the Extraversion—Introversion dichotomy of the MBTI personality inventory. The Learning Environment scale has some commonalities with the Sensing—Intuition dimension. The Risk Taking/Adventure scale adds an entirely new element.

These *Strong* scales are described on Worksheet 17 on page 80. Like MBTI dichotomies, they are based on opposite poles: Your score shows the strength of your orientation to one pole or the other.

Worksheet Directions

If you have taken the *Strong,* use your scores to mark your position on each of the scales on Worksheet 17. If you haven't taken the *Strong,* try to estimate where your scores might fall (the estimate will be just that, because the scoring for these scales is quite complex). If you are estimating your scores, ignore the numbers on the graphs; just show a preference for one pole or the other and the probable strength of that preference.

Worksheet 17 can help you see how your position on each of the scales might relate to your preferred modes of learning. The Risk Taking/Adventure scale, for example, may suggest to

WORKSHEET 17. My Learning Style in Relation to the *Strong*'s Personal Style Scales

WORK STYLE

Prefers to work alone; likes to work with ideas, data, or things; accomplishes tasks by independent action or thought

Prefers working with people as part of a group or team, or with one other person; enjoys helping others

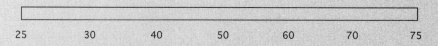

25   30   40   50   60   70   75

LEARNING ENVIRONMENT

Prefers practical learning environment; learns by doing; prefers short-term training; seeks training to achieve a specific goal or skill

Prefers academic environment; learns by lectures and books; willing to spend many years in school; seeks knowledge for its own sake

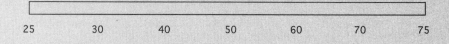

25   30   40   50   60   70   75

RISK TAKING/ ADVENTURE

Dislikes adventure and physical risk taking; likes quiet activities; prefers to play it safe

Likes adventure and physical risk taking; appreciates original ideas; enjoys thrilling activities; takes chances

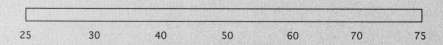

25   30   40   50   60   70   75

Source: Modified and reproduced by special permission of the Publisher, Consulting Psychologists Press, Inc., Palo Alto, CA 94303 from the *Strong Interest Inventory* Profile Report by Lenore W. Harmon, Jo-Ida C. Hansen, Fred H. Borgen, and Allen L. Hammer. Copyright 1996 by the Board of Trustees of the Leland Stanford Junior University. All rights reserved. Printed under license from Stanford University Press, Stanford, CA 94305. Further reproduction is prohibited without the Publisher's written consent.

you how much risk you want to tolerate in the process of learning. If you score toward the risk-taking pole, you may want to consider learning experiences that expose you to physical risk. These could include adventure treks, Outward Bound experiences, scuba diving, driving a motorcycle, or flying. If you score toward the plays-it-safe pole, you may prefer a safer environment in which to learn, such as a cruise, books, a guided tour, or a retreat setting.

Where Do I Go from Here?

Once again, as we have challenged you to do in other chapters, take the time to figure out what you have learned from these exercises. What do they tell you about the content of what you would like to learn and the process through which you learn best? Worksheet 18 will help you answer these questions.

Worksheet Directions

Use Worksheet 18 on page 82 to help you summarize what you've learned from the exercises in this chapter. After you've completed it, you can use it as a reference as you begin to identify and evaluate educational programs and opportunities.

Now it's up to you to investigate learning resources. We think you'll find this process much easier now that you have a clearer idea what you are looking for.

Other people are great resources. Ask your friends, acquaintances, and family members what resources they are aware of that match your learning profile. Go to your library or your local chamber of commerce and explain what kinds of educational resources you'd like to find. You may want to confine your search to the local area or you may be in a position to consider geographically broader options. Send for catalogues and brochures from universities, colleges, community colleges, and continuing education programs.

WORKSHEET 18. My Learning Profile

The Primary Content of My Learning	How I Prefer to Learn

Look in the Yellow Pages under training resources. Do an Internet search on the topic. Check the AARP Web site for relevant information. Try getting information from museums, social service agencies, and professional associations.

Ask your friends for the names of people they know whom they believe to be skilled in the area you want to learn about. Call these people and ask them how they learned, what training resources they respect, or what books they would recommend. Don't be afraid to pick up the phone. When people truly love their area of expertise, they talk about it eagerly and at some level hope that everyone will be interested.

In short, taking the first step toward doing something that will be rewarding for you can require considerable creative research. But somewhere the resource exists that will be *exactly* what you are looking for. If you get discouraged, consider experimenting with one subject area just to get a feel for what it's like to be a formal learner again—this experience can be a good confidence builder, and it may help you focus your interests.

7

FINDING NEW WAYS TO PLAY

You have always had special interests and hobbies, things that you do just for the sheer enjoyment of them. At this point in your life, however, you may have more time for leisure activities and recreation. If you are doing less in the realm of paid work, you may be able to devote more hours to those activities that you were only able to dabble in before. You can give more emphasis to the circle of life we call play.

Playing and having fun are often embedded in everything else we pursue, including work and learning. Many activities blur the traditional line between work and play. Consider, for example, a couple who turns a favorite hobby into a part-time business opportunity. They say it is fun and financially rewarding. Would you call it work or play?

In this chapter, play is whatever you find enjoyable or relaxing. We aim to stimulate your thinking about what leisure and play mean to you, and to help you broaden your range of options as you make choices about how to play.

Your Attitudes
About Play and Leisure

Attitudes are closely held beliefs about the way the world is. They often operate unconsciously, dictating our behavior or causing us to perceive events and possibilities through a single lens. Bringing attitudes out into the light of day gives you the freedom to critique and to choose. If I can articulate an attitude I have about something, I can ask myself if this is the way I want to continue to believe and behave. If I don't know my attitudes, they are my invisible coach.

Exercise 6 can help you become more aware of your attitudes about play. If possible, do it with someone who is quite different from you—someone, for example, with an MBTI type very different from yours.

EXERCISE 6: Exploring Your Attitudes About Play

Have someone read aloud to you, one by one, the list of words and phrases below. For each item, write down as quickly as you can everything the word or phrase reminds you of. Give yourself 20 to 30 seconds per item. Try not to think about the words too much before you actually do the exercise—the point is to free-associate.

Wasting time	Accomplishment	Time off
Play	Recreation	Enjoyment
Leisure	Hard work	Burnout
Fun	Duty	Recess

After you've written your list of responses, read them aloud and ask your partner to describe what your attitudes about work and play seem to be. Listen to the feedback. Think about how accurately it describes you. Which attitudes do you want to keep? Which do you want to change?

Your Orientation Toward Play and Leisure

The unconscious attitudes you have uncovered may be related to your *temperament,* another way of describing personality. According to the ancient Greeks, personality, or temperament, had physical origins. They used the metaphors of four Greek gods to distinguish one temperament from another. The four gods were Apollo, Dionysus, Prometheus, and Epimetheus. The myths say that Apollo had the gift of spirit, Dionysus the gift of

Table 6. The Four Temperaments

ISTJ	ISFJ	INFJ	INTJ
Temperament = SJ	Temperament = SJ	Temperament = NF	Temperament = NT
ISTP	**ISFP**	**INFP**	**INTP**
Temperament = SP	Temperament = SP	Temperament = NF	Temperament = NT
ESTP	**ESFP**	**ENFP**	**ENTP**
Temperament = SP	Temperament = SP	Temperament = NF	Temperament = NT
ESTJ	**ESFJ**	**ENFJ**	**ENTJ**
Temperament = SJ	Temperament = SJ	Temperament = NF	Temperament = NT

joy, Prometheus the gift of science, and Epimetheus the gift of work or duty. There is no psychological theory that has proved the existence of these temperaments, but in practice we have found that describing individuals according to a driving life force or temperament theme has considerable applicability to their lives. Therefore, we offer temperament here with the hope that you will find it a useful lens through which to view your results.

There are four temperaments among the 16 MBTI types; each suggests a different orientation to play, work, pleasure, and responsibility. Table 6 shows the temperament of each of the 16 types. Find your MBTI type in the chart and note the two-letter temperament code. Then read the description for your temperament in Table 7. It will tell you about how people with your temperament tend to approach play. (If you haven't completed the MBTI personality inventory, Worksheet 2, pages 25–26, offers a way of approximating your type. Or consult Appendix C of this book for providers who offer the MBTI.)

Each of the four temperaments has a particular life theme; you will learn about these in Chapter 9 when we look at balancing the four circles of life. For right now, just consider how well the description for your temperament fits your attitudes about play. You may also want to read about how the other temperaments approach play. Does one of them appeal to you more than your own? Have "shoulds" kept you from following another path?

Extraverted Play and Introverted Play

The Introversion–Extraversion dichotomy suggests an additional element about your orientation to play. Extraverts love to know and experience a little bit about as much as possible. Their leisure-time pursuits are often characterized by breadth and continual change. Introverts typically find great joy in knowing and experiencing things in depth. Their interests may be fewer in number but characterized by long-term commitment and intensity.

But preferences are not destiny. You have a choice: Either stick with your preference for depth or for breadth, or try out your opposite. If you are an Extravert, try choosing one area to explore in depth. If you are an Introvert, consider dabbling in a few things. By experimenting with different approaches to play, you may discover a new kind of joy.

Choosing Leisure Activities

There are no limits on what you might do or pursue. Unfortunately, however, people tend to fall into leisure-time ruts and lose sight of the diverse world that is open to them. We have found it helpful to use the *Strong*'s General Occupational Themes to stimulate people's thinking about leisure activities and broaden their leisure horizons. If anything, life after 50 is a time to explore all kinds of possibilities!

Table 7. The Temperaments at Play

NT	SP
To watch an NT type playing is to see intensity, determination, and an intent to improve his or her skill. If an NT takes up the game of golf, for example, he or she will mentally play and replay much of the game to figure out how to play better. NTs will often take a course in whatever the area of interest happens to be—stargazing, scuba diving, car racing, orchid growing, bridge, traveling, mountain climbing, or yoga. The NT wants to have as much knowledge as possible about his or her chosen areas of play. Despite their intensity, NTs are capable of thoroughly relaxing and enjoying themselves when at play. Their friends, however, may perceive otherwise. If you are an NT, you have probably had to withstand challenges from close friends and family members who think you never take a break. On the other hand, maybe it is true!	If you are an SP type, you have your own special approach to play. Living in the moment and playing as much as you can is often your life theme. Some say that the joy SPs find in playing is contagious. They often choose recreational activities and hobbies that require considerable energy. There is a freedom in the way SPs play that is quite different from the way NTs play. For an SP, work has to be fun, and learning should allow experimenting in the moment. SPs often have serial interests: Rather than following one course for a long period of time, they do something until it is no longer enjoyable. As SPs age they are often more bothered by their physical limitations than people of other temperaments. Yet they have the greatest ability of all of the temperaments to use humor and to find ways to enjoy themselves. They may discover ways to have sedentary adventures, since the urge to be active and live in the moment is always with them.
SJ	**NF**
The life theme for the SJ type is duty and responsibility. Therefore, work, commitment, doing things for the greater good of the community, and finishing responsibilities all must come before play. Ask SJs what they do for play or relaxation and they are likely to talk about something that is productive. If you are an SJ and are recently retired, it is especially important that you find a hobby or volunteer activity that provides you with the emotional feeling of being productive. The SJ will relax and find great enjoyment in leisure activities if he or she feels that the leisure time has been earned. If you have ever listened to Garrison Keillor's *Prairie Home Companion* and heard the news from Lake Wobegon, you have met the epitome of the SJ in the Swedes and Norwegians who populate this small fictional town. They can't just take off and enjoy themselves: they have to do something to deserve it first!	The life theme of an NF type is individual growth and development. NFs believe that relaxation and enjoyment are meant to be experienced because they form a natural part of human life. Each person has inner needs that must be nurtured and fulfilled, and these include the need for leisure and play. Like SPs, NFs can be very joyful in their play, but their joy flows out of the experience of being themselves. If you are an NF, your leisure-time activities are likely to be as diverse and complex as you are. Many NFs, particularly those who are Introverted, find reading and writing to be food for the soul. They need some inward-focused and reflective activities in their leisure time to be truly happy. NFs have known all their lives that a person needs to play and relax. If you are an NF, you may view NTs and SJs as too intense and work-bound.

On Worksheet 19 we have listed typical leisure activities that individuals who score high on each of the Themes often choose to do.

Worksheet Directions

Read through the items on Worksheet 19, marking or highlighting anything that piques your interest. Pay particular attention to the Themes in your Theme code, but don't neglect the activities associated with other Themes. (If you haven't taken the *Strong,* you can estimate your *Strong* Theme code by working through Worksheet 1 on pages 16–17.)

Even more than the life circles of work, learning, and relationships, play offers the opportunity to step beyond your established boundaries. Hobbies and leisure activities let you dabble in things for fun that you never thought you could or would pursue. There are no grades, no requirements, and no demands to be the best unless you impose them. You can have great fun plunging into something just to experiment.

The number of leisure-time pursuits is practically infinite. If you find our list too narrow, try browsing through special interest group areas on the Internet. You may be amazed at all the resources that exist. Or sit down with a group of friends over dinner and see how many interest areas you can add to our listing.

Your Way of Pursuing a Leisure-Time Activity

In addition to helping you identify enjoyable hobbies and leisure-time activities, your Theme code can help you understand how you can pursue a particular activity to get the most enjoyment out of it. Many leisure-time activities have diverse facets. They can be enjoyed and appreciated by people with very different sets of interests because they can be adapted to a person's particular inclinations. A person with Artistic interests, for example, will get satisfaction from photography

WORKSHEET 19. Leisure-Time Interests I Want to Explore

Realistic

Camping, canoeing
Flying
Woodworking
Crafts-related hobbies
Sailing, boating
Reading military history
Riding a motorcycle
Training pets
Fishing, hunting
Building models
Working on cars
Keeping fit
Restoring antiques
Gardening
Operating a ham radio
Home building projects
Pursuing the martial arts

Investigative

Solving math puzzles
Playing chess
Playing bridge
Playing board games
Going on study tours
Learning about investments
Building electronic devices
Inventing a product
Studying architecture
Playing software games
Reading science fiction
Learning about health
Doing crossword puzzles
Attending science fairs
Going on archaeological
  digs
Visiting science museums

Artistic

Writing
Playing an instrument
Performing in a musical
  group
Learning a language
Drawing, painting
Doing needlework
Dancing
Cooking
Antiquing
Following fashion trends
Making stained glass
Attending concerts, plays
Going to art museums
Decorating rooms
Acting
Photography

Social

Entertaining
Joining a club
Reading self-help books
Helping friends
Learning sign language
Teaching a religion class
Child care
Experiencing other cultures
Leading a study tour group
Reading romance novels
Being in a discussion group
Coaching children's sports
Meditation
Exploring spirituality

Enterprising

Following politics
Fund-raising
Competing in a tournament
Gambling
Leading a discussion group
Giving speeches
Reading biographies of
  leaders
Starting a business
Campaigning
Attending public meetings
Working with Junior
  Achievement
Coaching a team

Conventional

Cataloguing things
Tracking statistics
Using new software
Training pets
Working with computers
Assembling photo albums
Learning the history of a
  place before traveling
  there
Geneology
Collecting crafts or art
  objects
Managing investments
Organizing club activities

Table 8. Different Approaches
to Antique Restoration

Theme of Greatest Interest	Likely Emphasis
Realistic (R)	Doing the actual restoration work; repairing the furniture in addition to restoring the finish
Investigative (I)	Reading and learning more about antiques and how to recognize and restore them
Artistic (A)	Expressing creativity in choosing and restoring the antiques
Social (S)	Taking a class in furniture restoration and pursuing this activity with others
Enterprising (E)	Shopping for antique furniture; bartering or selling the pieces that you restore
Conventional (C)	Keeping track of the techniques used so as to have a record of how things work; cataloguing the collection

because of the way it allows him or her to express creativity, whereas a person with Social interests might pursue photography as a way of getting involved with people, either by photographing them or taking photography classes with others.

Restoring antique furniture is another good example. We have classified it under the Realistic Theme because it is most closely related to enjoying activities that are hands-on and concrete. But it can be greatly enjoyed by someone who has stronger interests in any of the other Themes, as described in Table 8.

Once you identify a new leisure-time activity, think about what your interests—as summarized by your Theme code—suggest about how you might most enjoy that activity.

Linking Play to Work, Learning, and Relationships

As you can see by reading over the list of activities on Worksheet 19 (page 91), almost any of these hobby areas could be turned into a volunteer activity or even paid work. And any of them can be the focus of learning or of an enlivened social life. In fact, if you are involved in an activity that is a particular passion, you may find real enjoyment from pursuing it in-depth in all four circles of life: work, learning, play, and relationships.

For example, a man we know has a passion for golf. Playing golf began as a leisure-time interest—it was integral to *playing* for him. Wanting to improve his game, he also pursued the sport avidly as a *learner* whenever he could. He attended golf schools, read extensively, and learned from the pros. Then he started offering people golf lessons in his spare time (just for fun, but it was a kind of volunteer *work*). Now he has a full-time business, teaching golf around the country, offering books and videotapes, and speaking to groups. That one passion eventually became the focus of all the circles of his life—and all after age 50!

You may discover your own ways of leveraging a source of enjoyment into work, learning, and/or relationships. Be creative and at least take risks in your daydreams. The circle of play offers many paths for balancing and integrating all the circles of life—a topic we'll address more fully in Chapter 9.

8

FOCUSING ON RELATIONSHIPS

Your second half-century offers many opportunities to reinvent the fourth circle of your life—the area of relationships. Changes in your work life, roles, and responsibilities likely mean that for the first time in your life you are (or will be) truly free to consciously choose with whom you will spend time, and what the nature of the relationships will be. The increased latitude you have in defining your interactions with others can allow you to find greater meaning and fulfillment in your life.

Your relationships may change in this phase of your life simply because you have more time than before. If you have worked long hours or spent a lot of time travelling, you might see the next few years as an opportunity to spend more time with those who are important to you or to get to know those who might become important. You may have close friends that you have not kept up with or family members that you have neglected in favor of other activities.

In addition, you may now have more freedom to relate to people in the way you choose. Many of your past relationships may have been constrained by the particular role—such as parent, supervisor, or employee—you had to play in the relationship. If these roles have changed, you may now be able to relate to those same people in different ways. If you are a parent, for example, you might not have been able to enjoy fully the fact that your children are now in or approaching adulthood themselves. Or you may have had many responsibilities at work that limited the nature or extent of your relationships with your colleagues.

As you redefine your relationships over the next few years, you will be able to address your own individual needs, perhaps to a greater extent than you were ever able to before. But to address your needs, you need to know clearly what they are. After years of attending to others' needs, you may not be closely in touch with your own! Your results on the *Strong* and the MBTI may provide you with some insights into what you need from relationships and interaction with others. With these insights you can then determine how to get those needs met.

Your Orientation to Social Interaction

Human beings are social beings, but each individual has a unique way of interacting with other people and a unique set of preferences and needs. Being aware of your particular orientation to forming and engaging in relationships will help guide you as you reinvent this area of your life.

One of the most basic aspects of your social orientation is whether you prefer Introversion or Extraversion. Extraverts gain energy from contact with a large number of people and thrive on frequent or constant interaction. Introverts prefer to interact with others one on one or in small groups and derive energy from reflection and time alone. If you have taken the MBTI or worked through Worksheet 2, pages 25–26, you know what your preference is.

If you have a clear preference for Extraversion, you might want to ask yourself if you have been engaged enough with others. If your answer is no, you might want to explore activities that would bring you into contact with larger numbers of people and give you the chance to expand your circle of friends and acquaintances. Depending on your interests, you might consider becoming active in large organizations, such as community or religious groups, or getting involved in politics. If you have been getting enough interaction with others, you can ask yourself if you want to continue to follow your preference or to explore your opposite by spending more time alone or focusing on deepening just a few important or primary relationships.

If your preference is for Introversion, ask yourself if you have enough time alone to recharge your batteries. You may be happiest having a few close friends and time for solitary activities. Consider fishing or hiking, or visiting museums and galleries with a special companion. If you have been getting enough time alone and already have good, intimate friendships with a few special people, you might consider exploring your opposite by interacting in groups or putting yourself in situations in which you can make new friends and acquaintances.

Another way of understanding how you approach relationships and relate to others is to consider your temperament. We introduced the idea of temperament in Chapter 7 when we looked at your orientation to play (see Table 6 on page 87 if you don't know your temperament). As a brief review, there are four temperaments—NF, NT, SJ, and SP—each of which includes four MBTI types. If your type is INFP, INFJ, ENFP, or ENFJ, for example, your temperament is NF. Each temperament relates to a life theme that has certain implications for relationships. Knowing your temperament can help you focus on the kinds of relationships that will be most satisfying for you. It can also help you identify potential challenges in your relationships and where you may need to develop different approaches. Study the description for your temperament in Table 9 on page 98. Evaluate how well it describes you and consider what you can learn from it.

Another way to understand the way you communicate with others is to look at the two middle letters of your MBTI type, which show your preferences for taking in information (Sensing or Intuition) and for making decisions (Thinking or Feeling). How you prefer to perform these functions shapes how you treat others and how they perceive you. There are four possible preference combinations for these dichotomies. Determine which of the four combinations matches your preferences, and read its description in Table 10 on page 99.

Table 9. Relationship Orientation of Each of the Four Temperaments

NT	SP
NT types tend to use time precisely, apportioning time fairly to individuals in their lives.	SP types respond quickly to the immediate needs of others and adapt easily to changing priorities. They tend to be troubleshooters and negotiators.
If you are an NT, you	If you are an SP, you
■ may assume your feelings are intuitively obvious and don't need to be voiced ■ may forget to consider others' commitments when you make plans ■ foster individualism in others and challenge others to think for themselves ■ can help others create a vision of what could be	■ enjoy relationships built around activities, not process ■ are willing to rush into situations that others hesitate to approach ■ are able to enjoy the moment and can teach others to do so as well ■ know how to play and get others to play ■ may shift relationships when your interests change
As an NT, one of your biggest relationship challenges may be expressing your feelings and showing sensitivity to the feelings of others.	As an SP, your biggest relationship challenge may be learning to develop or sustain long-term commitments.
SJ	**NF**
SJ types tend to be well-organized and well-grounded in their roles. They enjoy service, traditional relationships, and consistency.	Relationships are at the core of an NF type's being. NFs must have meaningful relationships to give their lives value and purpose.
If you are an SJ, you	If you are an NF, you
■ may become rigid about schedules and get impatient if you have to wait for others ■ like having well-defined roles for relationships ■ readily assume responsibility, which sometimes interferes with your ability to take time "off" ■ like to organize family events	■ spend time with relationships first, then attend to tasks ■ may neglect your own needs and easily get overextended ■ are good at inviting others to participate with you ■ value harmony and cooperation
As an SJ, your biggest relationship challenges may be developing a better sense of humor and being willing to explore the value of short-term or ambiguous relationships.	As an NF, your biggest relationship challenges may be learning to say no to others and to confront conflict rather than avoid it.

Table 10. How Preferences for
Sensing–Intuition and Thinking–Feeling
Affect the Approach to Relationships

	Sensing	Intuition
Thinking	**ST** If you prefer Sensing and Thinking, you ■ have a practical, matter-of-fact approach with others ■ trust logical analysis of the facts more than human emotion ■ deal with others objectively ■ may like being a role model, setting examples for others to follow	**NT** If you prefer Intuition and Thinking, you ■ are likely to be interested in the intellectually challenging aspects of relationships ■ may like to engage others in debate ■ are able to help others visualize abstract goals ■ are likely to engage in tasks with others
Feeling	**SF** If you prefer Sensing and Feeling, you ■ are likely to be sympathetic and friendly ■ enjoy situations in which you can express your personal warmth ■ prefer a predictable schedule and one-to-one social interactions ■ are good at collecting and remembering details about people	**NF** If you prefer Intuition and Feeling, you ■ enjoy sharing your personal warmth ■ want to be sure others' needs are met ■ are likely a good communicator and like interpersonal process ■ want harmony and dislike conflict

Source: Based in part on material in Hirsh, 1992.

After you read the description for your combination of preferences in Table 10, find that combination again in Table 11 on page 100. Here you will find suggestions for how you can develop more rewarding relationships and build your relationship skills and capacities. Some of the suggestions will have more relevance for you than others; pick one or two that speak to you.

Contexts for Interaction

So far we've concentrated on using your MBTI results as a guide for how to reinvent the relationship circle of your life. But your results on the *Strong* can be helpful in this regard too. Your interests can indicate contexts for social interaction in which

Table 11. Avenues for Relationship Development

ST	NT
Suggested ways of using your gifts ■ Share your experiences with children to help them learn and grow. ■ Share your problem-solving skills with adults. ■ Work in an advisory role for a community organization. **Goals for personal growth** ■ Develop skills for being more aware of others' feelings. ■ Learn to attend to others' emotional needs.	**Suggested ways of using your gifts** ■ Work with others to share your technical knowledge or expertise. ■ Help others brainstorm or be creative. ■ Engage with others in learning. **Goals for personal growth** ■ Develop skills for being more aware of others' feelings. ■ Learn to attend to others' emotional needs. ■ Stop assuming you know what others feel.
SF	**NF**
Suggested ways of using your gifts ■ Seek opportunities to engage others warmly while helping them with their day-to-day concerns. ■ Teach or care for younger people or children. ■ Work in a health care setting with children. **Goals for personal growth** ■ Evaluate when to say no to others. ■ Share your experiences and insights. ■ Become more comfortable in groups.	**Suggested ways of using your gifts** ■ Interact with adults in situations where you can help them understand underlying patterns ■ Show your appreciation for others' gifts. ■ Interact with others in a role in which you can give them freedom to be themselves. **Goals for personal growth** ■ Openly express your needs in a relationship. ■ Confront and resolve areas of conflict. ■ Learn to not take things so personally.

you feel most comfortable and at home. When you are pursuing your interests, you are following your heart, using your knowledge and skills. In these circumstances you are most able to "be yourself," relax, and open your life to those around you.

The general areas of interest represented by the Themes in your *Strong* Theme code are a good place to start in identifying the contexts and activities on which you might want to focus. Activities, organizations, clubs, volunteer positions, and learning experiences related to your Themes of greatest interest may

Table 12. Contexts for Social Interaction

Theme	Roles, Activities, and Environments to Consider
Realistic (R)	■ Passing along your technical knowledge or skill to others as a guide or mentor ■ Learning a new craft, skill, or recreational activity with others ■ Traveling, hiking, or camping in groups
Investigative (I)	■ Taking classes and engaging in intellectual discussion ■ Going on study tours ■ Fact-finding or doing research for organizations or groups
Artistic (A)	■ Taking art, photography, music, cooking, or crafts classes ■ Performing with a theater or musical group ■ Entertaining others or preparing meals together
Social (S)	■ Counseling or helping adults or children ■ Volunteering at a social service agency ■ Learning about others' lives
Enterprising (E)	■ Taking on community leadership roles ■ Doing volunteer fund-raising ■ Working on political campaigns
Conventional (C)	■ Helping a group get organized to accomplish its goals ■ Getting involved in a club related to one of your hobbies ■ Using the Internet to reach others with similar interests

provide good opportunities for meeting new people, deepening existing friendships, and/or satisfying your needs for social interaction. Table 12 offers a few ideas for each Theme.

For more ideas, consult the Basic Interest Scales on your *Strong* Profile. The areas in which you have the highest scores will suggest more specific activities and roles around which you can focus your process of relationship reinvention.

When you consider group activities in which you might want to be involved, think about what role you would like to play. Would you prefer a leadership role or a group member role? Are you more interested in learning about the lives of the individuals in the group or in supporting their efforts to do something? Are you happy working side by side with others on a project or activity that interests or intrigues you? Do you need to develop relationships with members of the group that allow you to address each person's individual needs and desires?

Reevaluating Relationships and the Role They Play in Your Life

Moving forward may require you to look backward first. Understanding what was unfulfilling about the past can be a catalyst for change in the present and future. At this moment in your life you have the opportunity to look back on your relationships with others, see what was missing, and take steps to change those relationships for the better. Are there people with whom you spent less time than you would have liked? Were you too busy being a wage earner, a boss, or a parent to enjoy a full range of friendships? Did you miss opportunities to do things with others that you would have liked to do?

Take the time to think carefully about the people in your life who are most important to you. If you knew that any one of them were going to die in the coming year, what would you want to make sure you did with them or said to them? Worksheet 20 on pages 104–105 allows you to evaluate all the important relationships in your life in this manner.

Worksheet Directions

You may want to complete Worksheet 20 column by column, first listing people and describing your relationships with them, and then considering the way in which you would change each relationship (if at all). Or you can complete it row by row, considering each relationship individually, first as it exists and then as you would like it to be. When you describe a relationship, you can consider the amount of time you spend with the person, the kinds of activities you share, the role you have in the relationship, the way you communicate, and how much of yourself you share with the person.

We encourage you to think of each relationship in terms of your needs and those of the other person. If, for example, you are a grandparent who is called upon mainly to train, discipline, and baby-sit, consider if you would rather focus on providing "fun" experiences for your grandchildren. Would you or your grandchildren get more out of the relationship if it were more focused on fun?

More generally, this exercise is an opportunity to ask yourself the most basic of relationship questions: What would you like to give, and to whom? What would you like to get back, and from whom? Remember that you have the power to define your needs and then later negotiate them with others.

We all play roles in life and need others to connect with, support, and love. In the end it is our willingness to share ourselves that gives meaning to our existence. Your human spirit gives life to others and is nurtured by those who love you. Reinventing yourself may give you the freedom to reshape and build important relationships and to really spend the time it takes to give to and receive from others.

WORKSHEET 20. My Relationship Action Plan

Relationship	My Present Commitments and Patterns	How I Want to Improve or Change the Relationship
Spouse/partner		
Children		
Grandchildren		
Parents		
Other relatives		

My Relationship Action Plan

Relationship	My Present Commitments and Patterns	How I Want to Improve or Change the Relationship
Close personal friends		
Casual acquaintances		
Neighbors and community members		
Work colleagues		
Other relationships		

9

ACHIEVING BALANCE IN YOUR LIFE

Many people today complain about not having enough time. They want more time for themselves, for doing what they really want to do, for leisure and recreation, for the important people in their lives. In our "sped up" world, time feels like a precious commodity.

We believe that having more time really means having better balance in your life. There's only so much you can do about "saving" time. The real issue is how you choose to split the time you have among the four circles of life—work, play, learning, and relationships. If one or two of the circles dominate your attention to the point that the others suffer, life may not feel as fulfilling as it could. Something important, something that nurtures your spirit, may be missing.

It may be that work has demanded too much of your time. What little time you have left you have devoted to family relationships, and both learning and play have been almost completely ignored. Perhaps raising children has meant giving most of your time to the circle of relationships. Or maybe you retired early and have found that doing nothing but play isn't as satisfying as you thought it would be. Whatever your situation, we hope that this chapter will help you find the kind of balance among the four circles that is best for you.

Is Your Life as Balanced as You Would Like?

The first step in finding better balance is determining how balanced or unbalanced your life is right now. The model of the four circles of life provides a good basis for this evaluation.

You give attention to each circle in the form of time, money, and emotional and physical energy. These are the resources you have to "spend." Different resources are devoted to each circle of life, but all your resources can be expressed in terms of time. Exercise 7 provides a way of figuring out and visualizing the way you split your time among the four circles.

EXERCISE 7: Time Budget

How do you use your time at this point in your life? Which of the circles of life gets the most attention? Which gets the least attention?

Draw a picture that shows how you apportion your time among the four circles of work, learning, play, and relationships. First, list the activities in your life that make up each circle and estimate the amount of time (per day, week, or month) you give to each activity. Then draw the circles, making each circle's size proportional to the amount of time you give that circle of life. You may want to list each activity within the circle in which it belongs.

When you consider which activities belong where, you'll have to make some decisions. If your work is lots of fun, for example, is it work or play? If you feel it is both, count the time you spend working as both work and play. Is an activity such as watching TV really play, or is it just a way to recover from work? If it is the latter, you may want to count it as work, not play!

Look at your drawing and consider these questions: What is satisfying to you about how you spend your time now? To which circle do you want to give more attention? What have you been ignoring or wishing you could do?

The Four Circles
in Your Life So Far

Before you begin creating your ideally balanced future, we'd like you to take a look back at your life from about age 20 up to the present. Think of your life so far in terms of the four circles: Which circle received the most attention when? When did you shift your focus from one circle to another?

To reconstruct your life in this way, it may help to think of it as a developmental process with distinct stages. Many authors, including Gail Sheehy and psychologist Erik Erikson, have written about life stages. A common theme in their writings is that people tend to experience their lives as a series of relatively lengthy periods of stability, or plateaus, connected by periods of transition. A transition can be smooth, or it can be traumatic and take the form of a crisis. During transition periods major questions tend to surface that can be unsettling or difficult to answer.

The plateaus correspond roughly to each decade of life, and the transitions to the ends and beginnings of each decade. Thus people typically go through a transition every 10 years or so. In the transition that often occurs around age 50, people become more aware of the advance of time and feel a need to find greater meaning in their lives. Their developmental challenge is to overcome the inertia of the previous decades and chart a new direction. Once they meet this challenge, they enter a plateau period during which they live their reinvented lives.

It often happens that each life plateau represents a focus on a particular life circle, and that each life transition involves a shift to a different circle of life. Thus the sequence of typical life stages makes a good framework for creating your life-circle history. We have provided this framework for you in Worksheet 21 on pages 110–111.

Worksheet Directions

For each transition and plateau on Worksheet 21, think about which circle or circles of life dominated your time and

WORKSHEET 21. My Life-Circle History

Age	Typical Developmental Task or Challenge	My Experience	The Most Important Circles of Life for Me
20	What do I really want to do?		○ work ○ learning ○ play ○ relationships
25	I'll show them I can do this on my own.		○ work ○ learning ○ play ○ relationships
30	Is this really the right choice for me?		○ work ○ learning ○ play ○ relationships
35	Let me work at being a success at what I have chosen.		○ work ○ learning ○ play ○ relationships
40	I don't have forever; is this all worth it?		○ work ○ learning ○ play ○ relationships
45	I have recommitted or found a new way to make a difference.		○ work ○ learning ○ play ○ relationships

My Life-Circle History

Age	Typical Developmental Task or Challenge	My Experience	The Most Important Circles of Life for Me
50	What haven't I done that I would like to do?		○ work ○ learning ○ play ○ relationships
55	I am having fun and finding meaning in my life.		○ work ○ learning ○ play ○ relationships
60	Can I come to terms with what I can't do or haven't done?		○ work ○ learning ○ play ○ relationships
65	I am expressing who I am.		○ work ○ learning ○ play ○ relationships
70	What do I want to leave as a legacy?		○ work ○ learning ○ play ○ relationships

☐ Transition   ☐ Plateau

attention during that period. The column of typical developmental tasks or challenges is there to help you remember the issues that might have defined each stage for you. Fill in each box in the "My Experience" column with a brief description of what you were doing at that stage of your life. In the right-hand column, note which life circle or circles were predominant. If no one circle assumed a prominent position, then note the four were in relative balance. Remember that the work circle has to do with whatever you chose for your life work or major work role, paid or unpaid. Also, don't worry about whether the ages in the chart match the exact ages at which you experienced transitions.

When you have completed the worksheet, study your life-circle history and think about the life choices you have made. What have you learned about balance? What patterns emerge? Has play ever been a big part of your adult life? Was learning in the forefront for a while, only to fade later on? Are there any life circles that have never received very much attention? What does this history tell you about what you would like to do in the future?

The Pull of Your Temperament

We have already looked at how your temperament—either SJ, SP, NT, or NF—tends to give you a certain orientation to playing (Worksheet 19, page 91) and relating to others (Worksheet 20, pages 104–105). Your temperament also plays a role in how you balance your life. It can predispose you to spend your time in a particular life circle. You need to be aware of this subtle pull so you can decide whether you are gravitating toward certain activities, roles, or responsibilities because you want to or because they are a habit.

Each temperament is closely associated with a different circle of life. Figure 4 shows these associations. Each temperament also has an "opposite"—a circle of life that a person with that temperament most easily ignores or downplays. In the figure, the opposite of each temperament is the circle of life directly across from it. Find your temperament in Figure 4

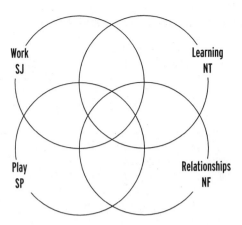

**FIGURE 4. Relationships Among the
Life Circles and the Temperaments**

and note which life circle is its mate and which is its opposite (if
you don't remember your temperament, look at Table 6 on
page 87).

Now look at Table 13 on page 114. It describes how each
temperament is attracted to its associated life circle and what
challenges that particular attraction poses. As you read the
description for your temperament, consider how well it fits you.
Does it capture what influences the choices you tend to make?
Also think about how much you have overlooked the circle of
life that is your opposite. You may not be drawn in that direction, but that's where self-discovery and life balance may lie.

The Role of Your Interests

Your interests also draw you more toward certain circles of life
and less toward others. They may attract you to the same circle
as your temperament or toward entirely different ones. In
either case you need to consider your interests when you seek
to achieve a better balance in your life.

Each circle of life is associated with one or two of the General Occupational Themes, as you can see in Figure 5 on page 115.
These associations are fairly loose; one circle of life can't
encompass all that is represented by one of the Themes. Yet it is

Table 13. Life Balance and the Four Temperaments

NT	SP
The NT type is drawn to the circle of learning. Following a life theme that emphasizes knowing, understanding, and intellectual competence, the NT will always be striving to improve, learn, and achieve a personal best. What the NT overlooks most is the circle of relationships. Because relationships involve more "being" than doing, NTs can feel a little restless in relationships and may make the mistake of not giving their important relationships enough attention for them to grow.	The SP type is propelled toward the circle of play. Since the life theme of SPs revolves around action and pleasure, they undertake many activities for sheer enjoyment. They tend to live in the present. What the SP may overlook is the joy that pursuing plans and working toward a long-term goal can bring. Certainly SPs will work diligently as long as the work is engaging, but they may neglect their values and what will give a long-term feeling of worth. In their focus on the present, they may fail to develop contingencies for their future.
For better life balance the NT may need to learn that ■ being is just as important as doing ■ spending time in relationships is not wasteful ■ emotions need time to express	For better life balance the SP may need to learn that ■ planning is not always incompatible with freedom ■ work can be central to building deep self-esteem ■ in-depth learning can be a source of satisfaction
SJ	**NF**
The SJ type, whose motto is "duty before play," gravitates naturally to the circle of work. Because the SJ's life theme revolves around responsibility, commitment, and being of service to others, it is often difficult for the SJ to consider doing something for himself or herself. Self-focused is the same as selfish in the minds of many SJs. The circle of work represents many "shoulds" for SJs, who have to figure out which ones to impose on themselves and which are only remnants of the past.	The NF type gravitates toward the circle of relationships. Whether working, playing, or learning, the NF values personal growth, appreciation, and support. Because the life theme of NFs centers on individual growth and personal development, NFs will long to find personal expression for their values in conjunction with others. And as the NF grows older, spirituality and values play a larger and larger part. The NF would rather be valued than judged; therefore, striving for achievement or sucess may feel too competitive or tough-minded.
For better life balance the SJ may need to learn that ■ there is room in life for more than work ■ you can have value without working ■ play needs more attention	For better life balance the NF may need to learn that ■ you can learn without being competitive ■ there is nothing wrong with trying to be the best ■ open debate and exchange of ideas are not destructive

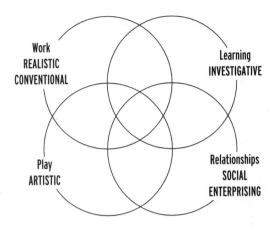

**FIGURE 5. Affinities Among the Life Circles
and the General Occupational Themes**

also true that a person with Investigative interests will be drawn to the circle of learning, for example, and that Social interests center on the life circle of relationships.

Recall your Theme code (see Chapter 2, page 17) and determine toward which of the circles of life your areas of strongest interest draw you. If your Theme code is more than one letter, your interests may attract you to two or even three circles of life, but the first letter of your code indicates your strongest attraction.

Think about your interests in terms of the circles of life to which you devote the most attention. Are your interests finding adequate expression? Is an imbalance among your life circles causing you to ignore an area of strong interest? (For example, you have neglected the learning circle in favor of the work circle, but you have strong interest in the Investigative Theme.) If all your interests aren't being expressed, consider devoting more time and energy to the life circle with which those interests are associated.

Now consider a somewhat different issue: Is a strong interest or narrow set of interests pulling you toward only one of the circles of life? If you have a great deal of interest in a wide range of activities, this situation isn't likely. People with broad interests generally find it easier to balance their activities among each of the circles of life. However, if you have fewer or more narrowly defined interests, they can be something of a barrier to achieving balance. If this is the case, the challenge for you may be to find ways to express your interests in different circles of life. If your interest in music, for example, has found an outlet primarily through leisure or play, then you may want to look for a way to express it through work (paid or otherwise). Or if your interest in science has been expressed through work, perhaps you can find an outlet for it in the area of learning.

How Your MBTI Type Influences Your Life-Balance Decision Making

How do you make major life decisions? What kinds of information do you consider? From whom do you take advice? What kind of process do you go through? All these aspects of making decisions are influenced by the preferences represented by the two middle letters of your MBTI type. If you know how these preferences shape your decision making, you'll be able to make better, more circumspect decisions about balancing the four circles of your life.

The second letter of your type—S or N—identifies your preferred way of taking in and understanding information: either Sensing or Intuition. The third letter—T or F—indicates your preferred way of making choices: either Thinking or Feeling. Sensing, Intuition, Thinking, and Feeling are all known as *functions*.

The two functions you prefer are your gifts. You use them both easily and naturally. But one—called the *dominant* function—has a greater influence on your personality because you use it more naturally and frequently. The other of your gifts, which you don't use quite as often as your dominant, is called your *auxiliary* function. If you are an Extraverted type, you use your dominant function in the external world—you *extravert* it and show it to others. If you are an Introverted type, you use your dominant function in your internal world—you *introvert* it and keep it to yourself.

Table 14. Hierarchy of Functions for Each Type

	Your Gifts			
Type	Dominant	Auxiliary	Tertiary	Inferior
ISTJ	Sensing $_I$	Thinking	Feeling	Intuition
ISFJ	Sensing $_I$	Feeling	Thinking	Intuition
ESTP	Sensing $_E$	Thinking	Feeling	Intuition
ESFP	Sensing $_E$	Feeling	Thinking	Intuition
INFJ	Intuition $_I$	Feeling	Thinking	Sensing
INTJ	Intuition $_I$	Thinking	Feeling	Sensing
ENFP	Intuition $_E$	Feeling	Thinking	Sensing
ENTP	Intuition $_E$	Thinking	Feeling	Sensing
ISTP	Thinking $_I$	Sensing	Intuition	Feeling
INTP	Thinking $_I$	Intuition	Sensing	Feeling
ESTJ	Thinking $_E$	Sensing	Intuition	Feeling
ENTJ	Thinking $_E$	Intuition	Sensing	Feeling
ISFP	Feeling $_I$	Sensing	Intuition	Thinking
INFP	Feeling $_I$	Intuition	Sensing	Thinking
ESFJ	Feeling $_E$	Sensing	Intuition	Thinking
ENFJ	Feeling $_E$	Intuition	Sensing	Thinking

E   used in the external world
I   used in the internal world

You also use the functions that aren't your gifts. They don't come as easily to you, but you do depend on them at times. One of these two remaining functions, called the *tertiary* function, is more accessible to you than the other; the least accessible one is called the *inferior* function.

Each type has a unique ordering of the four functions from dominant to inferior. Find the ordering, or hierarchy, of your functions in Table 14. Pay particular attention to which function is dominant for you and which is inferior, as these are the two we will be working with.

Your dominant function plays a visible role in your decision-making processes, including those that take place

Table 15. The Role of the Dominant Function in Making Life-Planning Decisions

Dominant Function	Types	Primary Questions and Considerations
Sensing	**ISTJ, ISFJ ESTP, ESFP**	■ What are the facts; what do I know about myself? ■ What would it cost me to make a change? ■ What is the problem I am trying to solve? ■ How do the experts suggest I go about this? ■ Who else could give me good information?
Intuition	**INFJ, INTJ ENFP, ENTP**	■ What are all my possibilities? ■ What can I imagine for my life in the future? ■ What if I could do anything I wanted? ■ What do trends tell me about the future? ■ Who else could help me be creative?
Thinking	**ISTP, INTP ESTJ, ENTJ**	■ What is the most rational and logical choice? ■ What are the pros and cons of each option? ■ What conclusion do the data suggest? ■ What steps should I follow in deciding? ■ Who could give me expert advice?
Feeling	**ISFP, INFP ESFJ, ENFJ**	■ What would make me the most comfortable? ■ What impact will this have on people I care about? ■ What fits best with my values? ■ What maximizes expression of my individuality? ■ Who could give me support or encouragement?

Source: Adapted from Myers, 1993.

during midlife transitions. When a function is dominant, it has a major impact on the kinds of questions or considerations to which you pay the most attention in making decisions. Find your dominant function in Table 15. The questions listed are those that are likely to be most prevalent in your thought processes when you make a major decision or choice.

When you make major life decisions—such as considering what role you want each of the circles to play in your life—don't rely on just your dominant function. It works well for you, but it can leave you blind to some important considerations. Make a special point to use the perspective of *all* of the functions. By

Table 16. The Inferior Function and Responses to Stress

Inferior Function	Types	Response to Stress
Sensing	**INTJ, INFJ** **ENTP, ENFP**	Get preoccupied or obsessed with unimportant details: overindulge in sensory pursuits, such as eating, drinking, shopping, or exercise
Intuition	**ISTJ, ISFJ** **ESTP, ESFP**	Imagine the worst and talk about how terrible things will be; get caught in one-track thinking; unable to see more than one option
Thinking	**ISFP, INFP** **ESFJ, ENFJ**	Become overly critical and blame others for anything that has happened; become self-centered and unable to listen to others
Feeling	**ISTP, INTP** **ESTJ, ENTJ**	Become very sensitive to criticism; express feelings in an extreme manner; unable to control anger, sadness, or impulse

Source: Based in part on material in Myers, 1993.

trying to answer all the questions in Table 15, you're more likely to make the best choice for you, as you will be rounding out and balancing your approach.

And what about your inferior function? We asked you to note what it is. That's because your inferior function plays a significant role when you are under stress, and stress often accompanies life transitions and major life decisions. Your inferior function operates unconsciously. It can exert its influence when you're under stress by causing you to respond inappropriately or to dwell on negative thoughts.

Find your inferior function in Table 16. Consider your likely response to stress, as described in the table. Do you ever notice yourself responding in this way?

Try to become more aware of your unproductive ways of dealing with the stress that comes from considering or making changes in your life. Learn to watch for signs that you are being inappropriately caught up in negative thoughts or actions.

Then, instead of getting lost in these behaviors, revisit the productive questions in Table 15 that could be asked by your inferior function. You may also want to interact with someone whose dominant function is your inferior function. That person can probably help you get out of the unproductive mode because of his or her ability to use the function productively.

Your Values and Life Mission

The four circles of life revolve around an anchor or centering element. That centering element is made up of your values. You can't create a well-balanced life without considering your values, which define your life purpose or personal mission.

Your values are so much a part of you that you may not be aware of them, especially as they relate to the universe of other possible values. You can get a much clearer idea of exactly what you value, and how strongly, by completing Worksheet 22.

Worksheet Directions

Worksheet 22 lists some commonly held values. Look them over and make additions in the blanks provided. Then go through the list and begin ordering the values according to their importance to you. Picking out your top five and your bottom five and ordering them within these subgroups first may help you rank them. Still it may be difficult to make choices among values that seem equally dear to you, especially if they seem to overlap. If this is the case, you can choose number five from your top five by thinking about which value you could "give up" as long as you could keep the other four. Then choose numbers four, three, and two in the same way.

When you have completed Worksheet 22, think about how you want to express or realize your most important values. Into which circles of life do they lead you? How do they fit together in your life planning? How do they translate into specific goals?

WORKSHEET 22. Clarifying My Values

_____ Achievement

_____ Family relationships

_____ Public recognition

_____ Financial reward

_____ Spiritual development

_____ Harmony

_____ Excitement and adventure

_____ Learning and knowledge

_____ Power and influence

_____ Fun

_____ Expertise and competence

_____ Security

_____ Personal growth

_____ Community

_____ Love

_____ Stability

_____ Creative expression

_____ Autonomy

_____ _____

_____ _____

_____ _____

My top five values in rank order

1. _____

2. _____

3. _____

4. _____

5. _____

My bottom five values in rank order

1. _____

2. _____

3. _____

4. _____

5. _____

You can begin to answer these questions by writing a statement of life purpose, a kind of personal mission statement. Many authors, including Stephen Covey (*The Seven Habits of Highly Successful People,* 1989) and Richard Leider (*The Power of Purpose,* 1997), point out the transformative power of creating such a document for yourself. It can be a very important part of reaching clarity about what you want out of life. Exercise 8 gets you started on your statement.

EXERCISE 8: Statement of Life Purpose

At the top of a blank sheet of paper, write "My mission in life is to . . . ." Then continue with whatever comes to mind. Start by listing parts of your mission if that's easiest. Write a little bit every day. Think it through, talk with someone close to you about your ideas, edit the ideas, and write your statement again.

Once you have anchored your four circles of life by writing a life mission statement and by clarifying your values, you are ready to build your ideal future! Exercise 9 is designed to help you create a picture or visual map of how you envision balancing the four circles of life.

When you have completed Exercise 9, you'll have two drawings of your circles of life—the picture of your present reality from Exercise 7 and the picture of time reinvented that you just created. With these two in hand you are ready to consider action steps. What can you do to move from present reality into your desired future? Write down one or two action steps that will help you create forward momentum. In the next chapter we'll discuss more ways of making progress on your journey.

It would be easy if your life-circle balancing act were a one-time activity. But it is not. Expect it to be a dynamic process. Anticipate taking stock of your present and future more than once in the next few years. Over time you'll find that some of the limiting factors change for you. Over time you will also discover new things about yourself.

EXERCISE 9: Reinventing Time

You can't speed forward, but you can imagine how life could be for you in the future. What kind of time and attention would you ideally give each of the four circles? Spend some time imagining what a typical month or year could look like. Look back at the life-circle history you constructed in Worksheet 21 (pages 110–111) for ideas.

Now make a drawing of the four circles as you did in Exercise 7 (page 108), except this time illustrate the kind of balance you would like to see for yourself in the future. As you did in Exercise 7, list within each circle the activities that would make up that circle, and show in the areas of overlap activities that are part of more than one circle of life.

After you have made your drawing, share your ideas with a friend or partner. Encourage this person to make a similar drawing. If he or she is a spouse or partner, make sure you talk about how to give each other space for the things that are important to each of you and how you want your activities to overlap.

10

EXPERIMENTING AND EXPLORING
The Journey of Reinvention

In the preceding chapters our purpose was to raise your level of awareness about yourself and the choices you have made. This chapter helps you launch the next phase of your journey of reinvention—using what you have learned about yourself to begin creating your ideal future.

As you explore and experiment, you may find surprise, sadness, disappointment, joy, guilt, contentment, fear, challenge, excitement, or grief. Acknowledge what you feel at each step of the way, and use this chapter as a guide and companion.

Coping with the Stress of Change

Reinventing yourself can (and should) be an all-consuming process. It will involve you in personal change at multiple levels: intellectual, emotional, physical, spiritual, and social. It will lead you into unfamiliar territory and make you question much of what you've taken for granted.

Stress is a natural result of this kind of change. As you continue on your journey of reinvention, then, you'll need ways of coping with the stress and keeping it from becoming a barrier.

Coping Strategies
People cope with stress by finding ways to replace depleted energy reserves and transform their attitudes about their

Table 17. Coping Strategies

Type of Strategy	Description
Cognitive	Engaging in reasoning and self-talk to achieve a more positive attitude. If you use this strategy, you tell yourself not to be so nervous, you consider what you have tried in the past, you project a positive outcome, or you comfort yourself with the knowledge that others have faced the same difficulties and persevered.
Physical	Relaxing or taking care of one's body to counteract the effects of stress or promote mental health and stress resistance. If you use this strategy, you may exercise, watch your diet, take dietary supplements, get extra sleep, receive therapies such as massage, or practice disciplines such as yoga.
Social	Seeking out contact with others to receive support, reassurance, or guidance. If you use this strategy, you may talk with friends, meet with others who are facing the same pressures, or take time for meaningful interaction. This strategy taps into the enormous supportive power of relationships.
Emotional	Expressing or releasing one's emotions. If you use this strategy, you may participate in an artistic endeavor, listen to an inspiring speaker, or express your feelings to a therapist or friend. Through such personal or creative measures deep feelings can be brought into the open.
Spiritual	Engaging in activities that nurture the soul. If you use this strategy, you may meditate, pray, read, or take part in any activity with deep personal meaning, such as creating works of art. Some spiritual coping strategies are pursued individually, others involve being part of a group, such as one that discusses values or spirituality.

Source: Adapted from Hammer and Marting, 1988.

ability to handle the circumstances. The methods used for coping can be grouped into five basic "coping strategies." These strategies are described in Table 17.

Read about the strategies in the table. Which do you use? Which have you never used? Which might you need when you face setbacks, disappointments, or painful realities during the reinvention process?

Table 18. Type and Coping Strategies

Type	Coping Strategies Used Most Naturally				
	Cognitive	Physical	Social	Emotional	Spiritual
ISTJ	✓				✓
ISFJ	✓		✓		✓
INFJ	✓	✓			✓
INTJ	✓				✓
ISTP	✓	✓			✓
ISFP			✓		✓
INFP		✓	✓		
INTP	✓				✓
ESTP		✓		✓	
ESFP	✓		✓	✓	
ENFP	✓	✓	✓	✓	
ENTP		✓		✓	
ESTJ	✓	✓	✓	✓	
ESFJ			✓	✓	✓
ENFJ	✓		✓	✓	✓
ENTJ	✓	✓	✓		

Source: Adapted from Hammer, 1991.

Your Coping Repertoire

All the coping strategies described in Table 17 are available to everyone, but each person tends to use regularly only two, three, or four. Research conducted by psychologist Allen Hammer (1991) suggests that the coping strategies used by people during times of stress is directly related to MBTI type. Your type predisposes you to reach first for certain strategies and ignore others.

Table 18 summarizes Hammer's findings, showing which strategies each type tends to use most comfortably. As you can see, some types have more strategies in their repertoires than others.

Notice which strategies your type tends to use. Do these seem to fit with what you do to cope with stress? Do you use some of the strategies that aren't listed for your type? Do you not use strategies that are listed?

Generally, the more resources you take advantage of the better. In fact, you may need to use all five of the coping strategies as you move through the process of reinvention. With all of them at your disposal you will be better able to deal successfully with stress and maintain your health, both psychological and physical.

Therefore try not to limit yourself to the strategies that are most comfortable for you. Use Table 18 as a guide for determining which coping strategies you need to work hardest at developing (those that are typical for your type will be the easiest to develop; those that aren't typical may be more of a challenge). Try working on one new strategy at a time and see how it works for you.

Making It Your Own Journey

It's important to navigate the process of reinventing yourself in a way that makes sense for you. One issue to consider is the influence that others may have on you. The advice you get from friends and family may be very helpful and supportive, but the choices you make have to come from within yourself. Asserting your independence may be especially important if most of your life decisions have been made with considerable influence, advice, or criticism from others. But independence doesn't necessarily mean making the journey alone. You may want to have someone accompany you who can encourage you to do your best thinking.

Another issue is how you want to travel on your journey. Your unique approach to life should be mirrored in the way that you go through the process of reinvention. After all, you want the reinventing process to be an exciting one that draws you into its spell. The last thing you want to do is set up a process for reinventing yourself that is dull and uninteresting.

Your areas of strongest interest, as identified by the *Strong*, can be a helpful guide for finding what's most comfortable and appealing. Each General Occupational Theme is associated with a certain way of approaching the reinventing journey, a way that fits with what motivates people who have that set of interests. Read about the approaches in Table 19 on page 130 that match your areas of strongest interest (as indicated by your Theme code). Consider how well these fit your style. Using the information in the table, decide what kinds of methods and activities make up your preferred approach to reinvention, and keep these in mind as you read the next section.

Steps in the Reinventing Process

The reinventing process is less intimidating if you think of it as a series of distinct stages or steps. You can tackle each step separately, accomplish what it requires, and move on to another, inspired by your progress.

We have identified six steps in the process. They are outlined in Figure 6 on page 131. Each step logically follows the previous one, forming a helpful framework that works for many people. But even though the steps are described in sequence, you aren't required to complete them in order. You can return to an earlier step if you want, skip over a step and return to it later, or begin a step without having completed the previous one.

The steps are arranged in a circle to denote the fact that the reinventing process never really ends. Your experiences help you learn about yourself; Step 6 experiences bring you back around to the beginning. Nevertheless, the steps we describe here will guide you in moving through the process and into creating the changes that make sense for you.

Both your MBTI preferences and your interests may influence how you pursue each step. If you have a preference for Judging, for example, you may have to push yourself to live with more uncertainty than you'd normally be comfortable

Table 19. Interests and Preferred Modes of Reinvention

General Occupational Theme	Preferred Mode of Pursuing Reinvention
Realistic (R)	■ Read how-to books. ■ Talk to others to get their advice. ■ Set tangible goals for each step of the way. ■ Establish a desired outcome. ■ Find someone who has done this well and talk to him or her.
Investigative (I)	■ Attend a seminar on career planning. ■ Take additional tests and inventories. ■ Consult with an expert. ■ Read as many books on relevant topics as you can. ■ Use research skills to learn about yourself and your options.
Artistic (A)	■ Attend a seminar on meditation. ■ Daydream while pursuing your favorite artistic activity. ■ Interact with others who have approached this creatively. ■ Write in a journal. ■ Express your feelings in art or poetry.
Social (S)	■ Participate in a group seminar to learn about yourself. ■ Find a supportive teacher or counselor to work with you. ■ Build networks and talk to friends about whom to contact. ■ Share your knowledge and ideas with others. ■ Ask others to comment about what they see in you.
Enterprising (E)	■ Seek out influential people for their advice. ■ Write a marketing plan for yourself. ■ Form a group and help lead others through the process. ■ Delegate some of the research tasks to others. ■ Pay attention to financial goals.
Conventional (C)	■ Keep notebooks that catalogue your skills and experiences. ■ Use the Internet as a tool for your research. ■ Buy a software program that systematically takes you through a life-planning process. ■ Create special charts and graphs that track what you do. ■ Keep a record of how you are using your time and money.

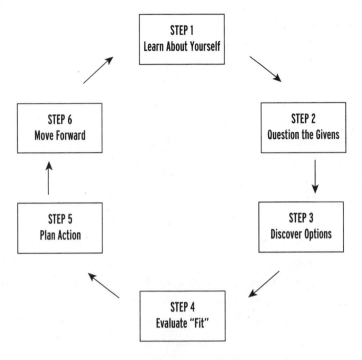

FIGURE 6.   The Steps of Reinvention

with. If you prefer Perceiving, on the other hand, you may need to force yourself to set deadlines and narrow your options.

Step 1: Learn About Yourself

Congratulations! You've already made significant progress in completing this step. All the previous chapters have been catalysts for helping you learn about yourself. You have been asking and answering questions about who you are, what's most important to you, what you have neglected in your life, and what you could be passionate about. Although you never really finish answering such questions, finding answers that ring true now is like having a ticket for the rest of your journey.

Both the *Myers-Briggs Type Indicator* and the *Strong Interest Inventory,* of course, are important tools for gaining self-knowledge. If you haven't completed either of these instruments, we still encourage you to do so. Estimating your scores gives you the opportunity to work through the exercises in this book, but that process cannot replace the richness of the inventories and the wealth of information they provide. Use the list of resources in Appendix C to find how you can take the inventories.

Other instruments can be helpful in Step 1 too. Standardized personality inventories, such as the *California Psychological Inventory*™ (CPI™) or the 16PF®, provide alternative ways of viewing who you are. You might also want to complete the *Career Factors Inventory* (available from the publisher) or an achievement or skills inventory, such as those detailed in Richard Bolles' *What Color Is Your Parachute?* (1998) or Jan Hagberg and Richard Leider's *The Inventurers* (1982).

While you are learning about yourself, you might enjoy employing techniques that have nothing to do with completing inventories and checklists. If you want more help with fantasizing about the future or using your creativity, you might consider reading Barbara Sher's *Wishcraft* (1983). If you have an active dream life and tend to remember your dreams (either in the middle of the night or first thing in the morning), keep a pad of paper by your bed. When you wake up, write down everything you can recall about the dream. Some of your dreams will doubtless give you clues about what is important to you. If you enjoy writing, keep a journal about your reinventing process. Record what you are learning, what it means to you, how you are feeling, and anything else that seems relevant to you. If you would love to try journaling but don't know where to start, consult one of the numerous how-to guides on writing journals that you can find in any bookstore.

Don't be afraid to let this first step be a long one. Six months is not an unreasonable length of time to spend learning about yourself. And don't let a false sense of closure prevent you from coming back to this first stage again and again or recognizing that it is always ongoing, even when you are focusing on a later step. As you explore options, try out new activities, or learn about what others have done, you will be learning more about yourself.

Finally, solicit feedback from people who know you. Not advice, feedback! Remember the grandmother in our first chapter. If she had listened to her children, she might have never pursued her dream of being an artist. Talk to a wide range of people. We often suggest that individuals find several feedback sources—among co-workers, friends, critics (yes, even critics have insightful things to say), and family members. Ask each one to comment on your strengths, seek their candid critique, and find out what they can imagine you doing. All this information is simply grist for the mill. You might be amused by it or inspired by it; remember that you are the only one who can decide what you want to take to heart and what you want to discard.

Step 2: Question the Givens

Nearly everyone is constrained in some way from doing exactly what they want. Rare is the person who has freedom from financial worries, perfect health, no ties to any geographic location, and no family or relationship commitments. But while some constraints are inevitable, people often let them have more power than they deserve. They think of their constraints as "givens," things they can't change, and work from there. Or they allow their apparent constraints to become excuses for inaction.

To keep your constraints from limiting your journey of reinvention—or preventing you from even embarking—you need to recognize what your constraints are and then question them. Some of your givens may actually be myths or mistaken assumptions. Some may be less constraining than you assumed.

The constraints people typically have fall into four primary categories: family responsibilities, financial limits, physical limits, and geographic ties. Any of them can box you in or act as boundaries on the range of possibilities you can consider for your life.

Before you can question your constraints, you need to be clear about what they are. We have provided Worksheet 23 on page 135 to help you identify and describe them.

Worksheet Directions

Consider each row of Worksheet 23 separately. List the constraints you have in each category and describe how each one seems to limit your choices. Here are some suggestions and questions to get you started:

1. *Family responsibilities.* Think about the primary relationships in your life and what you need to do to include them in your life planning. Do you have a partner with certain lifestyle demands? A relative for whom you need to provide some care or continuity? Grandchildren whom you wish to be near?

2. *Financial limits.* What are your needs in terms of income, ongoing saving for retirement living, and lifestyle choices? What resources do you have available for learning or starting a new venture? What do you need and what do you want?

3. *Physical limits.* What are you able to do given your overall stamina or energy level? What are your physical requirements in terms of climate and working environment? Do you have any disabilities?

4. *Geographic ties.* How tied are you to one section of the country or one area of the world? What holds you in one place or another? How distant are you willing to be from loved ones or work sites?

After you have identified and outlined your constraints, you can begin to question them. In Exercise 10 on page 136, we ask you to look at each area of constraint and challenge your beliefs about what is a "given." You may need to spend quite a bit of time reflecting on what the exercise brings to the surface. You may even want to discuss the exercise with a close friend or work on it with a counselor. Also consider completing the *Career Beliefs Inventory* (available from the publisher) as another way of identifying and challenging your assumptions.

WORKSHEET 23. Identifying My Personal Constraints

Type of Constraint	My Constraints in This Area and Why They Constrain Me
FAMILY RESPONSIBILITIES How family responsibilities and the needs of significant others affect my time and flexibility	
FINANCIAL LIMITS How my financial resources and earning power affect how I can work, what kind of lifestyle I can have, and what kind of enterprises I can begin	
PHYSICAL LIMITS How my health, physical abilities, and energy level affect where I can live and what I can do	
GEOGRAPHIC TIES How the area in which I live (and the strength of my ties to it) affect my opportunities and options	
OTHER Anything else that limits my options and influences my decision making	

EXERCISE 10: Challenging Your Constraints

Consider this hypothesis: Each constraint you have identified may be more of a self-limiting belief than a real choice or inevitability. Evaluate this possibility by asking yourself, reflecting on, and answering in writing each of the following questions.

Family responsibilities: To what degree are you just assuming that someone needs you? Are you living close to someone because that's your choice or because you don't feel you can do things any other way? Is the care you need to provide something only you can do, or can you create breaks from it by letting others take over? To whom are you the most responsible—the person for whom you are caring, or another family member who makes you feel guilty?

Financial limits: How real are your financial considerations? Have you sought out professional advice about what your needs are? Are you worrying too much about saving money when you could spend more on things that would make your life more enjoyable? Do you really need as much as you think you do for the future?

Physical limits: What makes you assume that something you dream about can't be done? What have others with the same physical limitations as you been able to do? To what extent are you selling yourself short because you don't want to make others have to accommodate you? What other coping mechanisms might there be?

Geographic ties: What keeps you in one place—a desire to stay in a single community or fear of starting up friendships all over again? How do you and your partner or significant other make decisions about where to live? To what extent do you really voice your opinion? What have you done to experience life in other parts of your country or internationally? Are you closing out options based on actual data or just feelings?

Step 3: Discover Options

The previous chapters have already helped you discover and entertain some new options for yourself. When you begin focusing on this step, your goal will be to further broaden your possibilities. When you complete Step 3, you should feel confused and a little overwhelmed—if you have done your homework well—since you should have generated more choices and possibilities than you could have imagined previously.

Most of us do a lot of research prior to making a major purchase or as part of learning about a topic. Yet we forget to use our research skills when it comes to charting our futures. Doing research does not mean just finding out what the library or the Internet has to offer. It means talking with individuals who have made similar life changes or interviewing people who are working in an area that holds some appeal for you. It means finding out who among your acquaintances knows someone who is doing something you have thought about doing, and then using your network to make a connection. It means reading current periodicals related to areas of interest to discover more about what is happening in that area. See Appendix B for a list of resources you might look for at the library or on the Internet.

If you happen to have a preference for Intuition or a high score on the Investigative Theme, the discovering-options step may be especially easy for you. Intuitive types thrive on brainstorming possibilities, and people with Investigative interests like the process of problem solving.

If your preference is for Judging, you need to give yourself a generous time frame for this step, so that you don't start narrowing your options too early. Judging types are most comfortable when they have reached closure, so they need to force themselves to live with more ambiguity than they would typically want to have. People with a Perceiving preference, on the other hand, may resist closure to the point of having difficulty eliminating some options that aren't worth continuing to explore. Therefore, if your preference is for Perceiving, establish the point when you will start narrowing the field of choices.

Others can serve as devil's advocates for you in this step, because it is here that you most need their challenges. They should be asking you things such as "Why are you discarding that option when it has such appeal?" and "You don't seem to be taking much risk in this process."

Step 4: Evaluate "Fit"

If you have done a good job in Step 3 of laying out an array of options, you will have considerable work to do in this step! It is during this step that you consider the options you have and evaluate them in light of your life-balance wishes, your values, your real constraints, and your desired lifestyle. Most likely you will have identified more paths that "fit" you than you can possibly follow. Therefore you will find yourself making difficult choices, weighing the impact of each, and making at least a tentative selection.

You may want to begin by returning to Chapter 9, "Achieving Balance in Your Life." Look at the work you did on your values in that chapter and rate each option for congruence with

---

EXERCISE 11: Virtual Reality

If you have an active imagination, you can "try out" in your mind each of the primary options you are considering for your life. If possible, make a recording of the script below so you can listen to it when you are feeling relaxed, or ask a friend to read it to you. Make sure you pause after each question to allow time for images to develop. You might try doing this exercise several times, once for each of your top possibilities.

Get in a comfortable position, close your eyes, and relax for a moment. Imagine you have chosen a certain option for your life and that it is a day in the future of that life path. It is early in the morning a few years from now. You are just waking up, stretching, and looking around you. Get a glimpse of your surroundings. Notice what the weather is like, who is there, and how you are feeling. Notice how much you are looking forward to the day. See yourself going through your morning routine and getting ready for the day. You feel especially positive about your upcoming day. See yourself heading off for your morning activities. Notice who you are with and what you are doing. Let yourself experience the day's events. Notice how you feel. See yourself during the lunch hour. Where are you? Are you talking with anyone? What kinds of people are around you and what are the surroundings like? Enjoy the rest of the day, experience the events of the afternoon, and involve yourself in the pictures you imagine. Now it is time for dinner and your evening activities. Pay attention to your surroundings again. Observe who is there, hear what is being discussed, notice how you feel. As you retire for the evening, you think back over your day. Notice how you feel about the day and how satisfied you are. When you are ready, open your eyes.

your values. You can test each option against how you feel and what impact the choice might have on others who care about you. And you can try Exercise 11 as a way of creating "virtual reality" around the options you are considering.

You can also learn more about the options you contemplate by talking with people who are doing similar things. Don't limit yourself to individuals who are your age and have gone through similar life choices. You have a goal of learning in depth about each option. People who are engaged in these activities now are your best source of information.

Allow yourself to experiment too. Making choices does not have to be a one-time activity, nor do you need to finalize a choice first and then see how it works later. Find a way to experience an activity, a work task, a subject you might want to learn, or a life-balance choice. You can try out a choice for fit, just as you might try on an article of clothing.

If you have a preference for Judging, you may have to push yourself to experiment because you would rather reduce the ambiguity and decide first. If you have a preference for Perceiving, you may need to set a time limit for your period of exploration so eventually you do find a first priority choice.

If your *Strong* results show a broad range of interests, you may be one of those individuals who makes serial choices. That is, you pursue one option for a few months or a few years and then you move to another. That does not make you indecisive or wishy-washy! Nor does it mean that you can't figure out what is important to you. It just means that part of your life satisfaction may derive from expressing many facets of yourself.

Another aspect of evaluating fit is figuring out just how much risk you are willing to accept. First determine the level of risk you're comfortable with—your score on the Risk Taking/Adventure scale on the *Strong* is a good reference point. Then rate each of your choices according to how much risk is involved, either in financial or psychological terms. Look at the options with the highest risk scores and think about what you know about yourself. Are you avoiding a choice just because you are uncomfortable with the risks it involves? Are you going for something only because it is the riskiest option and feels the most exciting?

Step 5: Plan Action

Just having an objective for your preferred future doesn't make it happen. Intellectually you know that, but many dreams have died for lack of a plan. We encourage you to put the plan on paper, including all of the steps you need to follow to realize the goal.

We have found it handy to use the art of backwards planning. That is, define first what you want to achieve and when. Then work backwards from that. For example, if you want to be in your own business within two years, then you need to find financial resources by a certain date. Or if you want to be able to paint watercolors well within two years, then you need to start taking the classes by a certain date. Just keep going backwards in your planning until you get to next week. What can you do next week that will take you one small step closer to your goal?

Some people are "natural" planners. If you prefer Thinking and Judging (that is, the last two letters of your type are TJ), you probably can't imagine starting anything without a plan. But be sure your reinvention plan has multiple routes to your destination and can be easily adapted to changing realities. On the other hand, if you prefer Feeling and Perceiving (the last two letters of your type are FP), you probably dislike planning. If this describes you, you may need to convince yourself about the need for a plan.

Knowing how you prefer to learn can also help with your planning efforts. Look back at Worksheet 17 on page 80 for how you placed yourself on the Learning Environment scale. (Or if you've taken the *Strong,* find that scale on your Profile.) If you like to learn by doing, you may want to ask someone who is good at planning to walk you through the steps. If you like to learn in an academic environment, you may benefit from taking a project management or life-planning class. If you score in the middle of the scale, do a little of both.

Many individuals find it helpful to use what we call *force field analysis* as they develop their action plans. For any object to move, the driving forces have to be stronger than the restraining forces. If the forces are in balance, the object doesn't move. People are the same as objects in this respect. Maybe you have tried to reach a goal and been frustrated by lack of progress. It may have been that the driving forces on you were balanced out by the restraining forces. Worksheet 24 on page 142 provides a framework to use in identifying the forces that drive you toward a particular goal and the forces that hold you back.

Worksheet Directions

When you consider forces within yourself in working through Worksheet 24, include your motivations and past experiences on the driving side, and such things as a lack of confidence, fear, and perfectionism on the restraining side. Driving forces in other people may come in the form of support and encouragement; restraining forces in the form of criticism and discouragement. Forces in your environment can involve finances, access to education, and community norms and values.

When you have painted a picture of what tends to move you and what keeps you from moving, you need to either strengthen the driving forces or negate the power of some of the restraining forces (or both). If you feel stuck and unable to figure this out on your own, find someone to help you imagine what you could do.

Finally, don't neglect contingency plans. These are your backup strategies for how you will handle various roadblocks or setbacks if they occur. Anticipating and planning for things that can go wrong gives you greater ability to handle any eventuality.

WORKSHEET 24. Forces Influencing My Ability to Achieve My Goal

My Goal Is: _____

	Driving Forces What helps me achieve my goal?	**Restraining Forces** What holds me back?
In myself		
In others		
In my environment		

Step 6: Move Forward

The primary focus in this step is on implementation. To transform your dreams into reality you will become fully immersed in making change happen.

Do the little things that speed your progress. Ask your friends, for example, to put some friendly pressure on you. Tell them your plans in great detail and then ask them to be your alter ego and support. Chances are that they will quiz you about your progress, be there to help you get back on track, and celebrate your accomplishments.

A mentor, guide, or travelling companion can provide real help while you are implementing your plan. The best guides are people who have made a major shift or transition in their own lives, and who are either very similar to you or very different (that is, with the same or the opposite MBTI preferences). If possible, find someone who has already attained your particular goal—such as turning a hobby interest into a business.

Make the implementation process interesting for you. Set up activities during this phase that help you express your strongest basic interests (look back at Worksheet 5 on page 38 for your rating of basic interest areas). If you intend to throw yourself into learning about business, for example, don't neglect your interests in other pursuits. Either give them an outlet too, or find ways to adapt their expression to your business-related goal.

Expect to experience some setbacks. Once in a while you'll take a few steps back when you hope to be advancing. Or events may occur in your life that seem to derail your progress. You know that making progress toward goals often feels jerky; don't expect it to be smooth. If you expect perfection, you'll be gravely disappointed. And on the other hand, if you anticipate failure, you'll be paralyzed into inaction. Keep reminding yourself how exciting your imagined future will feel.

Writing this book has been a journey for us. As we end our journey, we hope we have helped you begin or continue yours. We invite you to write to us and share your experiences. Being students of life changes and having great interest in how the *Strong* and the MBTI work for others, we look for ideas and feedback for our work with people like you. Good luck!

Appendix A
The Sixteen MBTI Types

These descriptions, oriented toward how people express their preferences in work situations, are adapted from *Introduction to Type® in Organizations,* Second Edition, by Sandra Krebs Hirsh and Jean M. Kummerow (Consulting Psychologists Press, 1990). Use the descriptions to learn more about your known type or to help you decide which type fits you best.

ISTJ

ISTJs are thorough, painstaking, systematic, hardworking, and careful with detail.

People with ISTJ preferences are likely to
- be adept at handling and managing details
- have things in the right place at the right time
- use experience and knowledge of the facts to make decisions
- respect traditional approaches and appreciate well-defined roles

ISTJs usually prefer to work in settings
- in which hardworking people focus on facts and results
- that are orderly and allow privacy for uninterrupted work

ISTJs may be irritated by others who
- don't follow through with plans and promises
- interrupt and talk too much

If not aware of their potential blind spots, ISTJs may
- expect others to conform to standard procedures and thus stifle innovation
- become rigid in their behavior and be seen by others as inflexible

ISFJ

ISFJs are sympathetic, loyal, considerate, and kind, and they will go to any amount of trouble to help those in need of support.

People with ISFJ preferences are likely to
- be painstaking and responsible with detail and routine
- expend effort willingly to serve others
- use personal influence behind the scenes
- follow traditional procedures and rules conscientiously

ISFJs usually prefer to work in settings
- that are calm and quiet and allow for privacy
- in which conscientious people perform a service for others

ISFJs may be irritated by others who
- set up ill-defined tasks
- get off track and don't follow their own agendas

If not aware of their potential blind spots, ISFJs may
- not be seen as tough-minded enough when presenting their views to others
- be undervalued because of their quiet, self-effacing style

ESTP

ESTPs are action-oriented, pragmatic, resourceful, and realistic individuals who prefer to take the most efficient route to getting something done.

People with ESTP preferences are likely to
- be enthusiastic, adventurous, and spontaneous
- notice and remember factual information
- take charge readily in crises
- seek action and immediate results

ESTPs usually prefer to work in settings
- in which fun is valued
- that are technically oriented and not bureaucratic

ESTPs may be irritated by others who
- are passive, unfocused, and unrealistic
- complain, whine, and negate

If not aware of their potential blind spots, ESTPs may
- appear blunt and insensitive to others when acting quickly
- sacrifice follow-through in favor of attacking the next immediate problem

ESFP

ESFPs are friendly, outgoing, fun-loving, likeable, and naturally gregarious.

People with ESFP preferences are likely to
- bring enthusiasm and cooperation to any occasion
- accept and deal with people as they are
- facilitate effective interactions among people
- ease tense situations by pulling conflicting factions together

ESFPs usually prefer to work in settings
- that are lively and action oriented
- in which easygoing people interact harmoniously

ESFPs may be irritated by others who
- are blaming, negative, and pessimistic
- fail to appreciate the differences among people and their unique contributions

If not aware of their potential blind spots, ESFPs may
- overemphasize subjective impressions
- spend too much time socializing and neglect tasks

INTJ

INTJs are independent, individualistic, single-minded, and determined individuals who trust their vision of possibilities, even in the face of skepticism from others.

People with INTJ preferences are likely to
- have strong conceptual and design skills
- work to remove obstacles to goal attainment
- love complex challenges
- conceptualize, design, and build new models

INTJs usually prefer to work in settings
- in which decisive, intellectually challenging people focus on implementing long-range visions
- that encourage and support autonomy

INTJs may be irritated by others who
- are slow to catch on or who dispute unimportant details
- don't finish what they've agreed to do

If not aware of their potential blind spots, INTJs may
- appear so unyielding that others are afraid to approach or challenge them
- be overly critical of others in their striving for the ideal

INFJ

INFJs trust their own vision, are insightful, and have deeply felt compassion. Seeking harmony, they exert influence quietly.

People with INFJ preferences are likely to

- have future-oriented insights about how to best serve human needs
- be able to organize complex interactions between people and tasks
- try to win cooperation rather than demand it
- work to make their inspirations real

INFJs usually prefer to work in settings

- that provide opportunities for creativity
- that are harmonious and allow time and space for reflection

INFJs may be irritated by others who

- are hostile, impertinent or don't appreciate others
- focus only on content, forgetting process

If not aware of their potential blind spots, INFJs may

- not be forthright with criticism
- be reluctant to intrude upon others and thus keep too much to themselves

ENTP

ENTPs are innovative, individualistic, versatile, analytical, and attracted to entrepreneurial ideas.

People with ENTP preferences are likely to

- view limitations as challenges to be overcome
- take initiative and spur others on
- apply logical systems thinking
- use compelling reasons for what they want to do

ENTPs usually prefer to work in settings

- that are change oriented and include competent people
- that reward risk taking

ENTPs may be irritated by others who

- refuse to look at new possibilities
- lack an achievement-oriented, "can-do" attitude

If not aware of their potential blind spots, ENTPs may

- be competitive and unappreciative of others' input
- overestimate how much they can get done

ENFP

ENFPs are enthusiastic, insightful, innovative, versatile, and tireless in pursuit of new possibilities.

People with ENFP preferences are likely to

- focus on possibilities, especially for people
- originate projects, action, and change
- want to be in charge of the start-up phase of projects
- become spokespersons for values relating to people

ENFPs usually prefer to work in settings

- with a participative, unconstrained atmosphere
- in which there are imaginative people

ENFPs may be irritated by others who

- are chronically pessimistic and have a narrow focus
- argue too much and do not allow others to contribute

If not aware of their potential blind spots, ENFPs may

- move on to new ideas or projects without completing those already started
- overextend themselves

ISTP

ISTPs are expedient, realistic, aware of facts, and not likely to be swayed by anything but logical reasoning. They are adept at managing situations.

People with ISTP preferences are likely to

- act as troubleshooters, rising to meet the needs of the occasion
- have a natural talent for working in technical areas
- prefer a cooperative team approach
- manage others loosely and prefer minimal supervision

ISTPs usually prefer to work in settings

- that are project-oriented and allow for hands-on experiences
- that support their orientation toward action and their desire for independence

ISTPs may be irritated by others who

- are contrary and illogical
- are overly emotional

If not aware of their potential blind spots, ISTPs may

- keep important things to themselves and appear unconcerned to others
- move on before prior effort bears fruit

INTP

INTPs are rational, curious, theoretical, abstract, and prefer to organize ideas rather than situations or people.

People with INTP preferences are likely to

- demonstrate expertise in tackling complex problems
- apply logic, analysis, and critical thinking to everything they do
- cut directly to the core of an issue, asking probing questions
- clarify information and present data in an impartial manner

INTPs usually prefer to work in settings

- in which independent thinkers focus on solving complex problems
- that are flexible and offer quiet

INTPs may be irritated by others who

- are redundant in their thinking
- are easily hurt or offended

If not aware of their potential blind spots, INTPs may

- focus too much on minor inconsistencies at the expense of teamwork and harmony
- turn their critical analytical thinking on people and act impersonally

ESTJ

ESTJs are logical, analytical, decisive, and tough-minded when they need to be. They are able to foresee problems and organize resources well in advance.

People with ESTJ preferences are likely to

- enjoy organizing processes and people
- follow through systematically to meet deadlines
- value competence and pragmatism

ESTJs prefer to work in settings

- that are organized and efficient
- in which hardworking people focus on doing the job correctly

ESTJs may be irritated by others who

- are constantly late, absent, or present but not participating
- are unprepared and don't follow up on tasks

If not aware of their potential blind spots, ESTJs may

- miss the wider impacts of their quick decisions
- overlook others' feelings and needs in working to get the job done on time

ENTJ

ENTJs are logical, organized, structured, objective, and decisive. They are natural leaders and builders of organizations.

People with ENTJ preferences are likely to

- design strategies for working toward broad goals
- deal directly with problems caused by confusion and inefficiency
- provide long-range vision to an organization
- take charge quickly and enjoy running things

ENTJs usually prefer to work in settings

- that reward decisiveness
- in which goal-oriented people work under an efficient system

ENTJs may be irritated by others who

- lack commitment to team goals
- lack a systems perspective and waste time and resources

If not aware of their potential blind spots, ENTJs may

- overlook people's needs in their focus on the task
- decide too quickly and appear impatient and domineering

ISFP

ISFPs are gentle, considerate, and compassionate toward others, and they have an open-minded, flexible approach.

People with ISFP preferences are likely to

- act to ensure others' well-being
- be cooperative, loyal, and hardworking
- rise to the occasion and adapt to what is needed
- gently persuade others by tapping in to their good intentions

ISFPs usually prefer to work in settings

- in which cooperative people quietly enjoy their work
- that allow them private, aesthetically appealing space

ISFPs may be irritated by others who

- talk too much, interrupt, or put down others and their ideas
- lack common sense or won't collaborate

If not aware of their potential blind spots, ISFPs may

- be overly self-critical and not critical enough of others when needed
- not see beyond the present reality to understand things in their fuller context

INFP

INFPs are open-minded, idealistic, insightful, and flexible individuals who want their work to contribute to something that matters.

People with INFP preferences are likely to

- be persuasive about their ideals
- draw people together around a common purpose
- praise others rather than critique them
- work independently to realize their visions

INFPs usually prefer to work in settings

- with a cooperative atmosphere, focused on values of importance to people
- that are flexible and not bureaucratic

INFPs may be irritated by others who

- won't admit when they don't understand an idea
- take themselves too seriously

If not aware of their potential blind spots, INFPs may

- allow their perfectionism to delay completion of tasks
- try to please too many people at the same time

ESFJ

ESFJs are helpful, tactful, compassionate, and orderly, and they place a high value on harmonious human interaction.

People with ESFJ preferences are likely to

- pay close attention to people's needs and wants
- complete tasks in a timely and efficient way
- keep others well informed
- work well with others, especially on teams

ESFJs usually prefer to work in settings

- in which people are appreciative and sensitive
- that are organized, friendly, and goal-oriented

ESFJs may be irritated by others who

- are passive and take no responsibility for solving problems
- play the devil's advocate

If not aware of their potential blind spots, ESFJs may

- avoid conflict and sweep problems under the rug
- not value their own priorities enough because of a desire to please others

ENFJ

ENFJs are interpersonally adept, understanding, tolerant, and appreciative, and they are facilitators of good communication.

People with ENFJ preferences are likely to

- enjoy leading and facilitating teams
- inspire change and growth in others
- have strong ideals about how people should be treated
- have enthusiasm and excitement about the future

ENFJs usually prefer to work in settings

- that are supportive and social, encouraging expression of self
- that are settled and orderly

ENFJs may be irritated by others who

- allow too little time for interpersonal connection
- are unprepared and show disrespect for others' time

If not aware of their potential blind spots, ENFJs may

- idealize others and suffer from blind loyalty
- take criticism too personally

Appendix B
Job Search and
Career-Planning Resources

There is a great wealth of information available to aid you in the job search process. With just a little effort you can find listings of current job openings, advice about résumés and interviews, and various resources to help you find opportunities and get hired. We have not attempted to provide an exhaustive listing of all the sources of this information (other authors have done that quite well). Instead, we have listed some major resource categories to stimulate your thinking about where to find information, and we have listed some specific sources within each category.

If you want to begin with a more complete listing, find the current edition of *What Color Is Your Parachute?* by Richard N. Bolles, published by Ten Speed Press. The workbook section in the back of that book is a compendium of information about career counselors, Internet resources, books, and other materials. You can even access Bolles' most current resource advice through the Internet (see the listing of Internet adresses on page 161).

Good research takes considerable time and energy. But remember that one source can lead you to another and each contributes to your understanding of the world of work.

If you come across any sources that you believe should be described in the next edition of this book, please contact us through the publisher. We will answer your mail.

Libraries

In libraries you can learn about types of jobs, industries, economic trends, and career planning. Many libraries also have sources of job listings and access to the Internet. Don't overlook the following two important sources of information in libraries:

- *Reference librarians.* These people are trained to help you find the information you are seeking. They often have incredible amounts of information about diverse topics available at their fingertips. They excel in doing special searches for patrons and they are your quickest guide to information on special topics.
- *Marketplace data.* Some of the most invaluable library resources are books listing the names and addresses of virtually all the organizations that exist in this country. Do you want to find a particular kind of organization in your hometown? Do you want the names of the major companies in an industry in which you are interested? Are you searching for hiring trends in your area? Reference librarians can locate such information for you in seconds.

Books

There are more kinds of jobs than you've probably ever imagined. A number of books may be helpful in expanding the range of possibilities you are willing to consider. Two of the best are listed below.

Gottfredson, G. D., & Holland, J. L. (1996). *Dictionary of Holland occupational codes* (3rd ed.). Odessa, FL: Psychological Assessment Resources.
This book contains 12,860 job titles keyed to the Holland codes on your *Strong Interest Inventory* profile.

U.S. Department of Labor. (1991). *Dictionary of occupational titles* (4th ed.). Washington, DC: U.S. Government Printing Office.
This book lists the same 12,860 job titles in the *Dictionary of Holland occupational codes,* with terse but thorough descriptions of the jobs. Available in every public library.

There are huge numbers of books that purport to be able to help you identify and secure suitable employment. Many of these are indeed potentially helpful. However, many are written for those with limited experience in the job market. Below we list some of the resources likely to be most helpful for the readers of this book.

Alternative America. (Ed.). (1991). Boston: Alternative America, Resources.

Berg, A. (1994). *Finding the work you love: A woman's career guide.* San Jose, CA: Resource Publications.

Bird, C. (1992). *Second careers: New ways to work after 50.* New York: Little, Brown.

Bolles, R. N. (1998). *What color is your parachute? A practical manual for job-hunters and career-changers.* Berkeley, CA: Ten Speed Press.

Cohen, L., & Young, D. R. (1989). *Careers for dreamers and doers: A guide to management careers in the nonprofit sector.* New York: The Foundation Center.

Community Jobs: The employment newspaper for the non-profit sector. Washington, DC: ACCESS: Networking in the Public Interest.

Crystal, J. C., & Bolles, R. N. (1974). *Where do I go from here in my life?* Berkeley, CA: Ten Speed Press.

Hagberg, J., & Leider, R. (1982). *The Inventurers: Excursions in life and career renewal.* Reading, MA: Addison-Wesley.

Jankowski, K. (1995). *The job seeker's guide to socially responsible companies.* Detroit: Visible Ink Press.

Miller, A. F., & Mattson, R. T. (1989). *The truth about you: Discover what you should be doing with your life.* Berkeley, CA: Ten Speed Press.

Millner, N. B. (1998). *Creative aging: Discovering the unexpected joys of later life through personality type.* Palo Alto, CA: Davies-Black.

Minority organizations: A national directory (4th ed.). (1992). Garrett Park, MD: Garrett Park Press.

Nivens, B. (1988). *Careers for women without college degrees.* New York: McGraw-Hill.

Sher, B. (1983). *Wishcraft: How to get what you really want.* New York: Ballantine.

Smith, D., & LaVeck, J. (Eds.). (1990). *Great careers: The Fourth of July guide to careers, internships, and volunteer opportunities in the nonprofit sector* (2nd ed.). Garrett Park, MD: Garrett Park Press.

Other People

Other people, especially close family members and friends who have known you for a long time, are often valuable and overlooked resources. Of course, there is some danger in going to them for advice. They may have preconceived ideas about what you should be doing or they may react with behavior that has become habit over the years. But if they are able to maintain objectivity, those who know you well can often provide valuable insights about you and can react helpfully to your ideas and thoughts about your future.

Here are some ideas about whom you might involve in your search:

- *Family members* (other than your parents) may have insights as deep or deeper than those of close friends. Their connections and advice may help point you in the right direction.
- *Parents* typically want the best for you. They will have especially keen insights into your younger days, insights which may point the way back to early interests that you have put aside. But be cautious about taking all of their advice or feedback. They may not know many important things about you.
- *Friends* can be great coaches, companions, and devil's advocates. Describe the role you would like them to play. Their networks can perhaps be used to help you set up informational interviews or job interviews. At a minimum they have a good perspective on you and your capabilities. Ask for their feedback and support.

- *Co-workers* may recognize well the skills that you have (whether you get to use them presently on the job or not), and they may share your interests too. If they happen to have found their current work through a systematic job search process, they may be especially valuable resources and guides. However, co-workers only know you in one setting and their perspectives may be limited.

Internet

Any attempt to provide a listing of resources on the Internet is automatically out of date before it is published. Nevertheless, the Internet is an increasingly important source of job and career information. If you run a search for "career planning" or "career counseling," you will find numerous hits (more than 10,000 of them), so the sheer volume of possibilities is mind boggling. In addition, when you visit a site, not all of the information you will find is either helpful or accurate. Just as with any resource, you need to be a good consumer. We find that it's best to start with a reputable site that is not trying to sell you anything (other than perhaps a book).

General information about careers, job searches, career planning, and where to find important information on the Internet is available on the following sites:

- Richard N. Bolles' Internet site at the following address: www.washingtonpost.com/parachute. This site is packed with information and even ranks other sites for content and helpfulness.
- The Occupational Outlook Handbook (1996 – 97) at http://stats.bls.gov/ocohome.htm. This site offers data and projections from the Bureau of Labor Statistics. A section on the jobs of the future is just one of many special sections provided.
- The American Association of Retired Persons (AARP) has a website that includes a section on jobs and career information. Their address is www.aarp.org. To find job bank listings, go to bulletin/webjobs.

- There are numerous sites where you can find job postings, announcements of job fairs, listings of companies that are hiring, and community resources. Many sites allow you to post your résumé and some even try to match available openings with your search parameters. Here are a few of those sites:

  www.iccweb.com

  for jobs with the federal government

  www.espan.com

  many professional and managerial job postings

  www.monster.com

  jobs, job fairs, and events related to specific occupations

  www.cweb.com

  professional, technical, and managerial jobs

  www.emory.edu/CAREER

  Emory University's unique career center "help desk"

  www.jobcenter.com

  free résumé posting; conducts searches for you

  www.ajb.us

  America's job bank

  www.occ.com

  America Online's career center

  www.careermosaic.com

  mostly technology jobs and technology companies

  www.careerpath.com

  a free service including ad searches from major news papers and employer Web sites

- The home pages of many corporations and organizations have a section on hiring and placement opportunities. If you know the name of an organization in which you are interested, try its home page as a starting point.

- Many Internet users join newsgroups. Those groups exchange information about special topics. While they are not meant to be a place for finding a job, they may help you find connections or network with individuals who can lead you to special resources, organizations, or people who are hiring. Use these to discover more about the kinds of organizations to which individuals with interests similar to yours belong.

Business, Trade, and Professional Organizations

If you have a particular interest, chances are there is at least one organization in your area to which people with that interest belong. Join the organization if possible and attend its events as a route to building your networks. To find out what business, trade, or professional organizations exist in a particular field, ask someone who is active in the field about his or her professional affiliations.

There are also volunteer groups whose mission it is to share the learning that they have acquired over the years. The Service Corps of Retired Executives (SCORE) and Retired Senior Volunteer Program (RSVP) are examples.

Community Organizations

Community and neighborhood organizations devoted to such diverse activities as neighborhood clean-up, recycling, and voter registration are always short of help and are an excellent source of volunteer opportunities.

If you are interested in activities with a social service orientation, consider schools, local hospitals, retirement homes, assisted living facilities, hospices, and detention centers or jails. Volunteers play an important role in each of these kinds of facilities. And the volunteers will usually say that they are the ones who benefit most.

Newspapers

Most local papers have sections devoted to upcoming events, meetings of special interest or community groups, and the volunteer needs of community organizations. Find out what is available locally. In addition, many newspapers have a website through which you can link to bulletin boards that post special community events. Obviously, you may also want to peruse the want ads for employment opportunities. However, if all you do is send out résumés, you are not likely to have much to show for your investment of time.

Yellow Pages

The Yellow Pages help you with categories of information. We suggest searching under specific headings, just like you would on the Internet. Also try these headings: Associations; Consultants—career; Career Counseling.

Religious Institutions

Many religious institutions have support groups to help their members find work or other meaningful activities. If your church, mosque, or synagogue doesn't, start one. Some religious institutions even offer career counseling resources on an individual or a small-group basis.

Appendix C
Taking the *Strong Interest Inventory* and the *Myers-Briggs Type Indicator*

The *Strong Interest Inventory* and the *Myers-Briggs Type Indicator* (MBTI) are both published by Consulting Psychologists Press in Palo Alto, California. Since the results of both inventories must be interpreted by a qualified professional, you cannot complete either inventory by ordering it from the publisher. Instead, you need to seek out an individual or an agency qualified to administer and interpret the instrument. Luckily, those individuals or agencies are easy to find, and their services are often quite reasonably priced. Here is a list of some places to look:

- *Your local college or university career counseling center.* Just tell them you are trying to locate a professional who administers and interprets the inventories individually or in a group setting.
- *A career action center.* Many communities have an organization that provides career counseling, job and career information, classes, and workshops. The counselors in these organizations are usually qualified to administer assessments.
- *Your church, synagogue, or mosque.* Many religious organizations have external resources with whom they contract to offer services to their members. In this way you may find a wide variety of individuals who are qualified to administer and interpret the MBTI, including ministers, trainers, counselors, team builders, social workers, and therapists.
- *The Yellow Pages of the phone book.* Look under several listings, including Career Counseling (careful, some of these are employment agencies); Counselors; Psychologists—licensed; or Social Workers.

- *Your state's psychology association.* Most have a referral network as part of their offerings and should be able to point you toward someone who is qualified to interpret the instruments.

- *The Association for Psychological Type.* This organization can provide assistance in locating a provider for the *Myers-Briggs Type Indicator.* The web address is: www.aptcentral.org; the phone number is 816-444-3500.

- *Career counselors on the Internet.* There are a number of counselors with websites who advertise their interpretation services for these instruments. For a fee, they send you the instrument, you complete it, and they return it to you with an interpretation.

References

Bolles, R. N. (1981). *The three boxes of life*. Berkeley, CA: Ten Speed Press.

Bolles, R. N. (1998). *What color is your parachute? A practical manual for job-hunters and career-changers*. Berkeley, CA: Ten Speed Press.

Covey, S. (1989). *The seven habits of highly successful people: restoring the character ethic*. New York: Simon & Schuster.

Hagberg, J., & Leider, R. (1982). *The inventurers: Excursions in life and career renewal*. Reading, MA: Addison-Wesley.

Hammer, A. (1991). Type and Coping Resources. Paper presented at a meeting of the Bay Area Association for Psychological Type, Stanford University, Stanford, CA.

Hammer, A., & Marting, M. S. (1988). *Coping resources inventory manual*. Palo Alto, CA: Consulting Psychologists Press.

Harmon, L., Hansen, J., Borgen, F., & Hammer, A. (1994). *Strong Interest Inventory applications and technical guide*. Palo Alto, CA: Consulting Psychologists Press.

Hirsh, S. (1992). *MBTI team building program*. Palo Alto, CA: Consulting Psychologists Press.

Hirsh, S., & Kummerow, J. (1990). *Introduction to type in organizations* (2nd ed.). Palo Alto, CA: Consulting Psychologists Press.

Holland, J. L. (1959). A theory of vocational choice. *Journal of Counseling Psychology, 6,* 35–45.

Holland, J. L. (1965). *A manual for the Vocational Preference Inventory*. Palo Alto, CA: Consulting Psychologists Press.

Holland, J. L. (1973). *Making vocational choices: A theory of careers*. Englewood Cliffs, NJ: Prentice-Hall.

Leider, R. (1997). *The power of purpose: creating meaning in your life and work*. San Francisco: Berrett-Koehler.

Myers, I. B. (1993). *Introduction to type: A guide to understanding your results on the Myers-Briggs Type Indicator* (5th ed.). Palo Alto, CA: Consulting Psychologists Press.

Sheehy, G. (1995). *New passages: Mapping your life across time*. New York: Random House.

Sher, B. (1983). *Wishcraft: How to get what you really want*. New York: Ballantine.

Additional Readings

Career and Life Planning Resources

Bergquist, W. H., Greenberg, E. M., & Klaum, G. A. (1993). *In our fifties: Voices of men and women reinventing their lives.* San Francisco: Jossey-Bass.

Birren, J. E., & Feldman, L. (1997). *Where to go from here: Discovering your own life's wisdom in the second half of your life.* New York: Simon & Schuster.

Brehony, K. A. (1997). *Awakening at midlife: A guide to reviving your spirits, recreating your life and returning to your truest self.* New York: Riverhead Books.

Byron, W. J. (1995). *Finding work without losing heart: Bouncing back from mid-career job loss.* Rainier, WA: Adams Publishing.

Cochran, C., & Peerce, D. (1998). *Heart & soul resumes: Seven never-before-published secrets to capturing heart & soul in your resume.* Palo Alto, CA: Davies-Black.

Dempcy, M. H., & Tihista, R. (1996). *Dear job stressed: Answers for the overworked, overwrought, and overwhelmed.* Palo Alto, CA: Davies-Black.

Elliott, C. H., & Lassen, M. K. (1998). *Why can't I get what I want?: How to stop making the same old mistakes and start living a life you can love.* Palo Alto, CA: Davies-Black.

Harkness, H. (1997) *The career chase: Taking creative control in a chaotic age.* Palo Alto, CA: Davies-Black.

Isachsen, O. (1996). *Joining the entrepreneurial elite: Four styles to business success.* Palo Alto, CA: Davies-Black.

Leider, R. J., & Shapiro, D. A. (1996). *Repacking your bags: Lighten your load for the rest of your life.* San Francisco: Barrett-Koehler.

Marshack, K. (1998). *Entrepreneurial couples: Making it work at work and at home.* Palo Alto, CA: Davies-Black.

Sheehy, G. (1984). *Passages.* New York: Bantam Books.

Stevens, P. (1983). *Stop postponing the rest of your life.* Berkeley, CA: Ten Speed Press.

MBTI Resources

Corlett, E., & Millner, N. B. (1993). *Navigating midlife: Using typology as a guide.* Palo Alto, CA: Davies-Black.

Isaachsen, O., & Berens, L. V. (1988). *Working together.* San Juan Capistrano, CA: Neworld Management Press.

Keirsey, D., & Bates, M. (1978). *Please understand me.* Amherst, NY: Prometheus.

Kroeger, O., & Thuesen, J. (1988). *Type talk.* Gainesville, FL: Center for Applications of Psychological Type.

Kummerow, J., & Hirsh, S. (1989). *Life types.* New York: Warner Books.

Lawrence, G. (1979). *People types and tiger stripes.* Gainesville, FL: Center for Applications of Psychological Type.

Martin, C. (1995). *Looking at type and careers.* Gainesville, FL: Center for Applications of Psychological Type.

Millner, N. B. (1998). *Creative aging: Discovering the unexpected joys of later life through personality type.* Palo Alto, CA: Davies-Black.

Myers, I. B., with Myers, P. B. (1980). *Gifts differing.* Palo Alto, CA: Davies-Black.

Page, E. C. (1983). *Looking at type.* Gainesville, FL: Center for Applications of Psychological Type.

Pearman, R. R., & Albritton, S. C. (1997). *I'm not crazy, I'm just not you.* Palo Alto, CA: Davies-Black.

Quenk, N. L. (1993). *Beside ourselves: Our hidden personality in everyday life.* Palo Alto, CA: Davies-Black.

Richardson, P. T. (1996). *Four spiritualities: Expressions of self, expressions of spirit.* Palo Alto, CA: Davies-Black.

Tieger, P., & Barron-Tieger, B. (1995). *Do what you are.* Gainesville, FL: Center for Applications of Psychological Type.

Strong Interest Inventory Relevant Readings

Borgen, F., & Grutter, J. (1995). *Where do I go next?: Using your Strong results to manage your career.* Palo Alto, CA: Consulting Psychologists Press.

Kise, J. A. G., Stark, D., & Hirsh, S. K. (1996). *Life keys: Discovering who you are, why you're here, what you do best.* Bethany House.

Montross, D. H., Leibowitz, Z. B., & Shinkman, C. J. (1995). *Real people, real jobs: Reflecting your interests in the world of work.* Palo Alto, CA: Davies-Black.

Peterson, L. (1995). *Starting out, starting over: Finding the work that's waiting for you.* Palo Alto, CA: Davies-Black.

About the Authors

SANDRA DAVIS lives and works in the Twin Cities of Minneapolis and St. Paul. She cofounded MDA Consulting Group in 1981 and currently serves as its chief executive officer. She spends the majority of her time working with leaders, teams, and organizations on processes related to development, change, and renewal. After receiving her Ph.D. degree in counseling psychology in 1973 from the University of Minnesota, Davis continued her interest in assessment instrumentation by coauthoring *A Guide to Using the CPI in Organizations* and by serving on the *Strong Interest Inventory* Research Advisory Board. She balances sometimes competing aspects of her life by pursuing musical, outdoor, and artistic endeavors with her family and through community service.

BILL HANDSCHIN followed his interests in science and biology into the laboratory. After receiving his M.S. degree in genetics and cell biology in 1974 from the University of Minnesota, he worked for a dozen productive (but not fully satisfying) years in research and clinical laboratories. In his early 40s, he began to prepare himself for a second career by earning a Ph.D. degree in psychology. His focus has been jobs, the people who hold those jobs, and the organizations in which those jobs exist. Handschin has worked with MDA Consulting Group since 1987, and he is an assistant professor on the adjunct faculty of St. Mary's University of Minnesota. At age 55, he has had 10 years of satisfying experience in his new career.